BIPOLAR ESSENTIALS

Practical Skills for Families & Caregivers

PATRICK GILLETTE MD
BRETTEN C. GORDEAU
JEFFREY HILLIER PHD

Published by Carma Publishing LLC, Lake Worth, Florida, USA

Orders may be placed through the website www.carmapubs.com or at your bookstore.

© 2006 with the authors

First printing July 2006

ISBN: 0-9769581-3-9
          978-0-9769581-3-0

The information contained in this publication is believed to be correct at the time of going to press. Neither the authors nor the publisher assume any responsibility for any errors or omissions herein contained. Opinions expressed in the book are those of the authors and are not necessarily held by the publisher. While this book discusses some legal, financial and medical matters, nothing published in this book should be considered legal, financial or medical advice. Readers must always consult a physician, attorney, accountant or other professionals who can assist them concerning matters related to the topic of this book.

Printed in the United States of America

Table of Contents

Preface   iii
Acknowledgments   vii
About the Authors   viii

1. An Introduction to Bipolar Disorder   **1**
What is Unipolar Disorder?   5
The Bipolar Spectrum   7
Bipolar Disorder in Children and Adolescents   8
The Caregiver's Role   10
Suicide   11
Comorbid Illnesses   12

2. Talking to Your Doctor   **13**
Preparing for Your Visit to the Doctor's Office   14
At the Doctor's Office   16
After the Visit to the Doctor's Office   19
How Often Should I Talk with the Doctor?   20

3. Symptoms and Diagnosis   **21**
Collecting the Family History   22
The Family's Role in Diagnosis   22
The Diagnosis of Bipolar Disorder   23
What are the Episodes in the Bipolar Spectrum?   28
Diagnosing Bipolar Disorder in Children and
    Adolescents (Early Onset Bipolar)   33
Misdiagnosis – the Reasons and the
    Consequences?   36
Consequences of Nondiagnosis   37
After the Diagnosis   38
Internet Resources   39
References   40

4. Time for Planning   **41**
Budgeting   49
More Planning   50
Safety   51
Planning for the End   52
Planning for You   53

5. **Therapies**   **55**
    Drug Therapy (Psychotherapeutic Agents,
      Psychopharmacological Agents)   56
    Electroconvulsive Therapy   63
    Psychotherapy (Talking Therapy or Counseling)   64
    Treatment for Children and Adolescents   67
    Other Treatments   69
6. **The Effective Caregiver**   **71**
    This is a Family Disease   74
    Being a Partner in Treatment   75
    Coping Methods: Things to Remember and
      Consider   76
    Suicide or Threat of Suicide   77
    The Disorder vs. the Person You Know?   78
    Positive Thinking and Realistic Expectations   80
    Recognize Impending Episodes   81
    Communicating with the Bipolar Patient   82
    Do You Really Want to Take It Personally?   84
    Helping: You Can or Cannot Do It   85
    Structure, Structure, Structure!   90
    Step Off and Step In   92
    If Children are in the Household   93
7. **Crisis Management**   **95**
    Time to Make the Crisis-Prevention Plan   96
8. **Caring for Your Bipolar Child and Adolescent**   **107**
    Education for the Bipolar Child and Adolescent   108
    Compliance with Therapy   111
    How to Manage the Behaviors You
      Should Expect   112
9. **Support**   **119**
    Internet Resources   121
10. **Scientific and Medical Basis of Bipolar Disorder**   **123**
    Brain Cells   126
    Neurotransmission   130
    Genetics and Bipolar Disorder   132
    Brain Abnormalities in Bipolar Disorder   134
Glossary   **137**

Preface

You have picked up this book because you are curious about bipolar disorder. You suspect that you may soon become a caregiver for a family member or friend with bipolar or a related disorder or they may be showing some signs, and you just want to know what to expect from this dreadful disease. We have written this little book for you. It provides good information, in an easy-to-read format, to everyone who wants to know more about what to expect from someone living with bipolar disorder. Having said that, this book is not for the patient, but for you as the caregiver, family member, or friend. The person afflicted with a mood disorder, such as bipolar disorder, should be under the care and treatment of their doctor or psychiatrist so we do not offer any medical advice, but provide the essential information that you will need to prepare yourself for your role as a caregiver. This book is for you because it is your life that will be altered significantly by taking on the role of caregiver to the person living with bipolar disorder.

As you read this book, you will realize that the diagnosis of bipolar disorder is frequently not easy. The condition is often misdiagnosed, especially in children and adolescents, and is often not diagnosed at all. As researchers and doctors learn more about the disease, they change their views on how it should be described, how it should be diagnosed, and how it should be treated. Older ideas have to be revisited constantly and doctors have to be re-educated to improve their skills and improve patient outcome. Most doctors now consider bipolar disorder to be a spectrum of disorders. That is to say, it is not just one disease, but an entire spectrum of possible disorders ranging between unipolar depression and mania, with symptoms of both, and with varying severity of both. It is important to recognize where in the spectrum the patient lies because their treatment will be different depending on the diagnosis. The wrong medications may make the condition worse, so we must be very careful with the diagnosis.

The onus for getting an accurate diagnosis is on the patient and their families. People do not like to admit that there is something wrong with them and there is a particular stigma against admitting that they may have a mental disorder. This is based on fear and ignorance that the patient must get beyond in order to receive effective treatment. Family members and caregivers must play a role in getting the patient to a primary care provider or psychiatrist as soon as they start to see abnormal moods and behavior in the patient.

In general, people fear the use of phrases like "mental illness" or "mental disease" because of the connotations they suggest. They do not want others to think their loved one is "crazy" or "mad" or that there is something wrong with their brains. It is a strange piece of the human makeup that can deal more easily (emotionally and physically) with a broken leg or diabetes, but the notion of being mentally ill is not as acceptable somehow. So let us dispel any notions here — however you want to describe it, bipolar disorder is a disease of the brain, an illness associated with mental functioning. The good news is that you are not alone. There are millions of people in the United States and millions more around the world with bipolar and related disorders. There is more good news. The symptoms can be treated with prescription medications and with lifestyle management so that the person with bipolar disorder can live a productive life. This is the main reason for you and the patient to seek a medical opinion as soon as you notice that there might be something wrong with the person's mood and behavior.

The Role of the Psychiatrist

Just as people do not want to admit to mental illness, they also do not like people to know they, or their loved one, are going to a psychiatrist. You must get beyond this way of thinking. A psychiatrist is a doctor who, because of their training and experience, is far more likely to give a correct diagnosis than the primary care provider. The psychiatrist will prescribe the medications and the therapy to help the patient cope with their disorder. For those diagnosed with bipolar I disorder, it takes, on average, 6 years between the first contact with the medical system and the receipt of a correct diagnosis. For those diagnosed with bipolar II disorder, it takes 11 years. So the sooner you get to an expert, the psychiatrist, and give an accurate description of the patient's symptoms, the sooner they will be treated and relieved of the burden of the disease on themselves, yourself, family members, and friends.

There is No Cure, but There is Treatment

There is no known cure for bipolar disorder. What causes bipolar disorder and what triggers the manic and depressive episodes is also not known. What *is* known is that there is a strong genetic (hereditary) component to the disease, so that if parents or other family members have been diagnosed with bipolar disorder, you should be vigilant for the same or similar symptoms in their children. On average, people with bipolar disorder will die earlier than the "normal" population. This is useful to know when planning for the future.

There are many medications for the treatment of the symptoms of bipolar disorder. The primary care provider or psychiatrist will help you to find the right ones for your loved one. However, it is essential that the treatment plan be followed or relapses will occur. It is equally essential that the patient has the benefit of a caregiver to watch over them, to look for the telltale signs of bipolar manifestations, and to take care of them in their time of need. The role of the caregiver is not an easy one, but with good planning and armed with knowledge, we believe that your life can be made a little easier and, perhaps, even rewarding.

You, the caregiver, should expect that the person with bipolar disorder will be dependent on you eventually and, for this reason, your role as the caregiver is integral to the development of any plan of care for the patient. Therefore, we want to help you to understand what you should expect in your new role.

We have kept this book short by design. We want you to get the essential information in an easy-to-read format. We have provided a Glossary to help with the words that may be unfamiliar to you, and we have provided some references and Internet sites to help you to follow up and learn more. For those who will not read the whole book, we have repeated information on suicide, children with bipolar disorder, and the need to maintain medications several times, albeit in slightly different ways. We update the information in this book on a regular basis so that you will always have the most recent information as new ideas become known to us and as the research and medical communities make progress.

We welcome your feedback and suggestions, and you can contact us easily from the www.carmapubs.com website or by e-mailing us at publisher@carmapubs.com.

Acknowledgments

In writing this book, we have compiled information from many sources. We have read avidly; we have had many conversations with experts, patients, and caregivers; and we have the benefit of our own professional and life experiences. We want to thank all of you who have enhanced our knowledge of this terrible disease, whether you were aware of your involvement or not. We thank Barbara Caras for helping to make the book what it has become.

This book is dedicated to
all the caregivers who give so much
to care for those who are unable to care for themselves

About the Authors

Patrick Gillette, MD, CMD, is a physician in private practice at Medford Internal Medicine - Providence Medical Group in Medford, Oregon, where he specializes in internal medicine and geriatrics. In addition, he is the Director of the Mood and Memory Center of Southern Oregon and Senior Staff Physician at the Clinical Research Institute of Southern Oregon. Dr. Gillette also is Assistant Medical Director of Providence Medford Medical Center Hospice.

Dr. Gillette is a certified medical director and a member of several professional organizations including the American Geriatric Society and the American Medical Directors Association. He is also a member of several advisory boards and committees including the Advantage Advisory Board at Johns Hopkins University in Baltimore, Maryland, and the Providence Medford Medical Center Ethics Committee.

Bretten C. Gordeau is a co-author of the best-selling *Alzheimer's Essentials: Practical Skills for Caregivers* and is a memory-impairment specialist who has worked directly with hundreds of brain- and memory-impaired patients, their families, and caregivers in long-term and day care settings. He has spent the past 10 years working within neurology, neurosurgery research, and publishing. He holds seats on various boards of directors for neurodegenerative disorders. He attended Harvard and Cambridge Universities and completed his surgical science studies at the University of Miami Medical School Campus.

Jeffrey Hillier is a co-author of the best-selling *Alzheimer's Essentials: Practical Skills for Caregivers* and received his

PhD in neuropharmacology from the University of Bath, England. He has held senior management positions in several of the world's leading publishing companies and is a founder of Carma Publishing.

Other books for Caregivers:

Alzheimer's Essentials

To order any of our books or
for an update on all books from Carma Publishing go to
www.carmapubs.com

1. An Introduction to Bipolar Disorder

Bipolar disorder is one of the most severe forms of mental illness and is a relatively common disease that has been diagnosed in millions of people worldwide, and probably has been misdiagnosed or is undiagnosed in millions more. Some studies have shown that as many as 70% of bipolar patients have been misdiagnosed at least once and the vast majority of those were diagnosed with depression. It is the same disease that was once called manic-depressive illness and it is a disorder in the functioning of the brain.

The term "bipolar" comes from the distinct feature of the disease when the person cycles from one pole (mania) to the opposite pole (depression) and back. This change in mood, cycle, or mood swing can last for hours, days, weeks, or months. When the change in mood occurs frequently, at least four episodes within a 12-month period, it is referred to as "rapid cycling" and is more common in women and children than men. Some people experience multiple episodes within a single week or even within a single day. Rapid cycling tends to develop in the later stages of bipolar disorder.

Bipolar disorder is a very serious, long-term disease that has no cure, and the bipolar person must receive treatment (medications, counseling, and psychiatric help) and make lifestyle adjustments (living in routine(s), taking care of oneself physically, recognizing when mood changes are occurring, understanding triggers) to be able to manage their lives. To keep bipolar disorder under control, patients must stay on their medications and other therapies even during the periods when they are well. Bipolar disorder has a high rate of recurrence and if untreated, has an approximately 15% risk of death by suicide. Those who are most seriously affected by the disease can expect to be hospitalized several times during the course of their illness. On average, the bipolar person will die 7–8 years younger than those in the general population, independent of suicide. It is the third leading cause of death among people aged 15–24 years.

Bipolar disorder is a burden on families and on society because the person with bipolar disorder needs help from their caregiver, family, friends, and doctors all the time. It has been estimated that in the United States, the total annual societal cost of bipolar disorder may be as high as 45 billion dollars. Those people suffering from bipolar disorder also have a higher incidence of a variety of other medical conditions, such as diabetes, heart disease, thyroid disorders, etc. These are called "medical comorbidities" and they often get in the way of making the diagnosis of bipolar disorder.

Bipolar disorder is characterized by the unusual changes in mood, energy, and the ability to function displayed in the two extreme states of depression and mania. While everyone has good days and bad days, the person with bipolar disorder experiences very high "ups" in the manic phase and very low "downs" in the depression phase. The person with bipolar disorder is severely impacted by the disease, not knowing what to expect from one day to the next as their mood swings back and forth between manic episodes and depression. It can be difficult to diagnose and is often missed completely. The person may suffer for years before they receive a correct diagnosis and treatment. The important fact to recognize is that bipolar disorder is a disease, a long-term illness that can be treated by medications and lifestyle management. If left untreated, the bipolar person's life will be completely affected, leading to poor performance in school or work, bad behavior, lack of personal hygiene, sexual promiscuity, financial instability (spending binges), sleeplessness, aversion to receiving treatment (medication and therapy), difficult relationships, poor health, and even death by suicide (in severe cases).

It is not a new disease. Historical records indicate that many people — famous politicians (Abraham Lincoln, Winston Churchill, Teddy Roosevelt), authors (Tolstoy, Dickens, Balzac, Woolf), composers (Beethoven, Schumann, Handel), and others — exhibited the symptoms of bipolar disorder. That they went largely untreated and still survived and performed well is testament to the fact that it is possible to live with bipolar disorder, although people devastated by the disease is more the norm.

There are varying statistics in the medical and scientific literature about the incidence of bipolar disorder in the general population. The variation seems to be caused by the way in which the disease is diagnosed. While there are guidelines for diagnosis, some doctors will have a looser interpretation and others will have a tighter interpretation. An average figure for the prevalence of bipolar disorder is that about 2.3 million adults over the age of 18 in the United States have it and there are roughly equal numbers of men and women with the disease. The first episode in males tends to be a manic episode, while the first episode in females tends to be a depressive episode. The number of children and adolescents diagnosed with bipolar disorder is not known because the studies have not been done. However, it has been estimated that up to one-third of the 3.4 million children and adolescents with depression in the United States may actually be experiencing the early onset of bipolar disorder.

The cause of the disease and its symptoms of mania and depression are unknown. However, research has shown that there is a genetic predisposition to bipolar disorder. This does not mean that if someone has the gene they will get the disease, but that if something else triggers the gene, perhaps stress, then there is a good chance they will suffer from bipolar disorder. The symptoms seem to be triggered by imbalances of neurotransmitters in the brain that affect the regions of the brain responsible for mood, resulting in unusual mood swings and behavior. Some imaging studies suggest the involvement of structural abnormalities in the amygdala, basal ganglia, and prefrontal cortex of the brain. A more detailed account of the scientific and medical basis of bipolar disorder can be found in Chapter 10.

There is no fixed time in a person's life when bipolar disorder may manifest. It can develop in children, adolescents, adults, or late in life, although it is most frequently first diagnosed in late adolescence or early adulthood. Only a doctor can provide adequate diagnosis of any signs or symptoms, and whether they are indeed symptoms of mania or depression.

Substance abuse (alcohol and drugs) is a serious problem for the bipolar person because not only do alcohol and drugs possibly affect the functioning of the brain to exacerbate the bipolar symptoms, but they can also negatively impact the usefulness of medications. About half of bipolar patients will experience alcohol or drug abuse at some time during the course of their illness.

<u>What is Mania?</u>
In adults, mania manifests as increased activity; less need for sleep; overly euphoric mood; racing thoughts; and forceful, rapid speech.

Mania in children and adolescents may be quite different, exhibiting irritability and destructive tantrums.

<u>What is Depression?</u>
Depression manifests as difficulty in concentrating, sadness, anxiety, feelings of worthlessness, and loss of interest in normal activities.

Bipolar patients are depressed three times more than they are manic, 37 times more in depression for those with bipolar II disorder (see below for description), and the depressed phase of the illness results in more hospitalizations than the manic phase.

Depression accounts for nearly all of the suicides in patients diagnosed with bipolar disorder.

What is Unipolar Disorder?

Before we move on to discuss bipolar disorder in more depth, it is useful to explain that there is a disease described as unipolar disorder, unipolar depression, or clinical depression. This is the disease most commonly known as "depression". Unipolar disorder does not have the cycling between mania and depression; there is only depression characterized by a persistent depressed mood. It is important to understand that there are two diseases that share the symptom of depression because there can be significant consequences if diagnosed incorrectly. Some of the medications prescribed for unipolar disorder can exacerbate the symptoms of bipolar disorder and the ways in which these two diseases must be managed are quite different.

If you have any doubts about the diagnosis, ask the primary care provider why they have diagnosed unipolar and not bipolar disorder.

There are many reasons for a person to feel depressed from time to time, and this is quite normal. They may just be fatigued or feeling sad about a life event; or a depressed mood may be the result of relationship problems or work problems; or grief from a relative, friend, or family member sick or dying. It can also be the result of a normal physiological function, such as premenstrual syndrome or postpartum depression. Drug abuse frequently has side effects of depression when coming down from the effects of the drug.

Depression can also be the side effect of another illness, such as diabetes or Parkinson's disease. However, if the depression or depressed mood persists, it is time to consult the doctor. The signs to look for include loss of energy, poor concentration, lack of interest in normal activities, poor appetite, disturbed sleep or insomnia, indecision, irritability, anxiety, loss of hope, social withdrawal, thoughts of self-harm, and a generally low mood.

People suffering with unipolar disorder may appear to others as miserable, with reticent or monosyllabic speech, slumped posture, downturned mouth, and furrowed brow.

Unipolar depression is a serious clinical problem that is relatively common. It has been estimated that as many as 12% (roughly 36 million) of people in the United States are affected by depression, although it is also known that many sufferers remain undiagnosed and go through their lives without the treatment they need. There are many antidepressant medications available and most people respond favorably to these medicines (medications are discussed in detail in Chapter 5). Despite this, it has been estimated that three-quarters of all people diagnosed with depression will have a recurrence of the disease within 10 years. Because unipolar disorder can be difficult to diagnose, it is important that you recognize all of the symptoms and make sure that you tell the primary care provider. If you feel that your loved one's symptoms are not getting better with their current treatment and their doctor does not want to try something new, do not hesitate to see another provider to get a second opinion.

The treatment for unipolar depression will depend on the severity of the disease. For example, milder forms may be treated with psychotherapy alone while a moderate or severe diagnosis may dictate medication, psychotherapy, and psychoeducation.

The Bipolar Spectrum

The bipolar spectrum is often described as consisting of four disease states: bipolar I, bipolar II, cyclothymia, and bipolar disorder not otherwise specified (NOS). These disease states are differentiated by the severity of symptoms and episodes of mania and depression.

What is Bipolar I Disorder?

Bipolar I disorder is the more severe form of the disease and is characterized by "a distinct period of abnormally and persistently elevated, expansive, or irritable mood, lasting at least 1 week (or any duration if hospitalization is necessary)." The typical mood will include some of the following symptoms: more talkative than usual, inflated self-esteem, decreased need for sleep, distractibility, agitation, excessive involvement in pleasurable or high-risk behaviors. If a person has at least one episode of mania any time in their life, they have bipolar I disorder.

What is Bipolar II Disorder?

Bipolar II disorder is less severe and may be misdiagnosed as unipolar depression if the patient, caregiver, or doctor do not notice the signs of hypomania (hypomania is similar to mania, but less severe). Bipolar II disorder is characterized by one or more depressive episodes accompanied by at least one hypomanic episode.

The problem of diagnosis seems to be in detecting the difference between the hypomanic mood and the person's normal mood. The roles of the caregiver and the patient are very important when making the initial diagnosis. Their knowledge and awareness of any changes in mood or behavior that have occurred, and their ability to pass the information on to their doctor is crucial in order to make an accurate diagnosis. Changes that might occur include increased irritability, unusually energetic, unusually talkative, fleeting thoughts, easily distracted, trouble concentrating, less need for sleep, more involved in high-risk activities, or more involved in pleasurable activities (sex, shopping). The key to these symptoms is that they are unusual for the patient and are not part of their normal behavior. Changes take place that family members, friends, and others will notice.

What is Cyclothymia?

A third disorder, cyclothymia (also known as minor cyclic mood disorder), involves periods of hypomania and mild depression, but they are shorter, less severe, and less regular than in a bipolar II diagnosis. Symptoms last from a few days to a few weeks and are separated by short periods of normal mood. While less severe than in bipolar II disorder, the symptoms may be sufficient to disrupt the person's life and impact negatively on school, work, or social relationships. About 30% of people diagnosed with cyclothymia go on to develop bipolar II or bipolar I disorder. Cyclothymia is relatively common, affecting 0.4–1.0% of the population and occurs equally in men and women. The more common symptoms of cyclothymia are discussed further in Chapter 3.

What is Bipolar Disorder Not Otherwise Specified (NOS)?

A larger group of people (larger than bipolar I, bipolar II, and cyclothymia) demonstrate milder or different forms of episodic mood disturbances. These people are often not helped or their condition is made worse by antidepressant therapy. Because there is no other diagnosis yet defined, they are classified as bipolar disorder NOS.

Bipolar Disorder in Children and Adolescents

As we have noted above, there is a genetic component to bipolar disorder. Children of parents with bipolar disorder should be monitored carefully for signs of the disease during their childhood and later in life. It has been estimated that a child who has one parent with bipolar disorder has a 15–30% risk of developing the disorder. If both parents suffer, the risk increases to 50–75%. If any of the emotional or behavioral signs of bipolar disorder are seen in a child, you should immediately seek out a doctor who is specialized in childhood mental disorders because the diagnosis is difficult to differentiate from normal childhood mood swings and other disorders, such as ADHD (Attention Deficit Hyperactivity Disorder). In particular, bipolar disorder and ADHD are often confused in children because they have similar symptoms, such as periods of depression and a tendency to be distracted easily. It is essential to get a correct diagnosis because a misdiagnosis can lead to the child being treated with the wrong medications, possibly making the condition worse. Caregivers should watch and note changes in the child's moods and behavior, and report all such changes to the doctor. Any mention of self-harm or suicide is a clear sign that the child should be evaluated immediately. If the doctor is not experienced with childhood mental disorders, get a referral to an expert. It is important that children and adolescents are diagnosed early in the course of the disease so they can receive the proper treatment and medication.

The child with bipolar disorder can exhibit extreme symptoms, raging out of control for hours. They often experience rapid mood swings between mania and depression many times a day, although there will be a few periods of normal mood and behavior between the manic episodes and depression. In the manic phase, they are more likely to be irritable and prone to destructive outbursts. When depressed, there may be complaints of headaches, stomachaches, fatigue, poor performance in school, poor communication, and extreme sensitivity to rejection or failure. The bipolar child tends to be risk seeking and has grandiose thoughts with a nonstop flow of ideas. In adolescents, depression manifests differently than in adults. It is typified by anger, irritability, rebellious behavior, and drug use. Drug use is common in the bipolar child or adolescent, and the use of drugs can even be a symptom of bipolar disorder in children.

Bipolar children and adolescents have special educational needs that should be addressed by teachers, special education teachers, parents, and doctors in order to evaluate them and determine their educational requirements based on the particular manifestations of their disease and medications. Federal law requires that children who suffer from bipolar and similar disorders be accommodated in public schools and caregivers should take whatever action is necessary to make sure that the child receives the education to which they are entitled. More details on education for the child or adolescent with bipolar disorder can be found in Chapter 8.

The Caregiver's Role
It is unusual for a person to recognize the symptoms of bipolar disorder themselves, especially since the manic phase (i.e., the telltale symptom of bipolar disorder) makes them feel good. A more likely scenario is that a family member or friend will notice the changes in mood and behavior that may signal the need for a visit to the doctor for a checkup, and to receive an appropriate diagnosis and treatment regimen. If you are the family member or friend, you may need to encourage them to make an appointment with their doctor. If it proves difficult, you can make the appointment for them and accompany them to the appointment. Your presence will support them and the doctor will appreciate the information you can give about the mood and behavioral changes in the patient. When you have listened to the doctor's diagnosis, and if it is a disorder in the bipolar spectrum, you can also play a very valuable role by continuing to watch over the patient, monitor their moods and behaviors, encourage them to take their medication and make doctor and therapist visits, and generally support and help them in the difficult times.

The role of the caregiver is essential to enable the bipolar person to live as normal a life as possible. The emotional support you can provide, the good companion and friend, the one who can offer them hope, is how your role will benefit them, particularly in their worst moments. In Chapter 6, we have provided tips and tools for the caregiver that will help you to help your patient while making sure that you do not neglect yourself while you take on this role.

The role of caregiver to the bipolar patient is not easy. It requires commitment of your time and resources, and it requires an understanding of the disease, the patient, and how to deal with the problems you will be facing. The mood swings, when they occur, will demand your attention and your time to nurse the patient through their difficulties. Caregiving can have a negative effect on your own health as you struggle to cope with the burden. You may become stressed, depressed, emotional, overly critical, and even hostile to the patient. Your role as caregiver is not to be taken lightly. In this book, we provide tips, tools, and information to support you in order to make your own life easier while you take care of your loved one.

Suicide
Suicidal tendencies are not unusual in the bipolar population and almost always manifest when the person is deeply depressed. The tendencies usually occur early in the course of the illness so caregivers need to be particularly vigilant and aware at this time. Signs that a person may be contemplating suicide may be blatantly obvious, such as the person talking about suicide or writing a suicide note, putting their legal and financial affairs in order, or putting themselves in harm's way. Signs that may be less obvious could be that the person feels like a burden on their family, feels hopeless and helpless, and abuses alcohol and drugs. If any of these signs occur, immediate action is required and you should inform their doctor and therapist.

Knowing something about the patient's family history will benefit you in your suicide watch, since a family history of suicide is a major risk factor for suicidal behavior. Other risk factors include the severity of depressive symptoms, rapid cycling, alcohol and drug abuse, and the early age of onset of the bipolar disorder. If any of these risk factors are present in your patient, you must be extra vigilant and watch for any signs that they might be suicidal or want to harm themselves.

Comorbid Illnesses
A comorbid illness is another illness that occurs at the same time as the bipolar disorder. Comorbid illnesses are very common in bipolar people; 50% or more of those with bipolar disorder will have a comorbid illness that can complicate the diagnosis and the treatment of the disease.

Among the most common comorbid illnesses for the bipolar patient are other mental illnesses, such as anxiety disorders (post-traumatic stress disorder and obsessive-compulsive disorder), panic, and alcohol and substance abuse. The risk of a heart attack is doubled in people that have suffered at least one episode of depression, and depression has also been found to increase the risk of diabetes, stroke, bone loss, and possibly cancer.

2. Talking to Your Doctor

One of the primary responsibilities of the caregiver is to act as the go-between for the doctor and the patient. The caregiver provides information to the doctor about the patient and assists the patient in following the doctor's orders. In most cases, the best caregivers for people with bipolar and other mental disorders are those who have known them the longest, probably a spouse, parent, significant other, or family member.

The diagnosis of bipolar disorder can be very difficult for many primary care providers, especially if they have had little direct experience with the disease. Even with psychiatrists, it is not uncommon for bipolar disorder to be diagnosed incorrectly as depression (unipolar) or ADHD. This makes it even more important that you communicate effectively with the doctor to obtain an accurate diagnosis and to make sure that you are informed of all the options for therapy. (We provide information on diagnosis in Chapter 3 and on therapy in Chapter 5.) If the primary care provider is not very familiar with bipolar and related disorders, you should ask to be referred to an expert in this area.

Health care today is much different than it was 20 years ago. Doctors are busier than ever and they have limited time available, so communicating effectively with the doctor is more important than it ever was. You may wait for an extended amount of time both in the waiting room and exam room, and once you do see the doctor, your visit may be no more than 15 minutes. Because time is so limited, it is important that you be prepared. Communication is the sharpest tool you have available to you and how well you are able to talk with the doctor may affect the care of the person with bipolar disorder. The relationship between doctor and caregiver should be one based on the sharing of information and working together to make the best decisions about the patient's health, resulting in the best care being provided.

Preparing for Your Visit to the Doctor's Office
People, especially children, with bipolar disorder can behave normally, be polite, well mannered, and charming during a visit to the doctor. In these circumstances, it will be very difficult, if not impossible, for the doctor to diagnose the patient accurately. Therefore, you should plan for more than one visit to the doctor until you have a diagnosis. You know there is something wrong, so it is up to you to persist until the primary care provider sees the same symptoms that you see.

Involving other family members or friends familiar with the patient's mood and behavior changes may help you to be more accurate and focused, leading to a more productive discussion with the doctor. By having someone visit the doctor with you, they act as another set of ears and can act as a second voice when relaying complicated health information back to the family or to each other. It will be helpful to the doctor and the communication between all the family members if one person, usually the primary caregiver, serves as the main contact and informant. This person should plan on being at all of the appointments with the doctor.

Focusing on the current state of the individual with suspected bipolar disorder and their general health condition will help to prevent misunderstandings. Asking questions and focusing on relevant items may encourage the doctor to take more time with you. Do not make the doctor guess or come to conclusions; be precise and clear. Do not deviate and speak with the doctor about your own personal issues. You, as the caregiver, are there to convey the messages that relate directly to the patient's current emotional and mental state. Taking time to speak of unrelated issues will take up the minutes you have to discuss the relevant topics with the physician. If you need to discuss your individual issues, it is best to speak with the practice's nurse or social worker as they generally are there to support the family and caregiver(s). The more information you share, the better the doctor will be able to figure out the best diagnosis and treatment options (see Chapter 3 for a more in-depth discussion).

The best way to make the most of the limited time you will have with the doctor is to come to the appointment prepared. Make your lists of questions and prepare the information you will give to the doctor with a friend or family member a few days before the appointment. Include the following:

o A family history of mental disorders, no matter how trivial you think they may be. Especially include any family members who have been affected by depression, placed in mental institutions, or have attempted suicide.

o Gather both over-the-counter (cold medicines, vitamins, etc.) and prescription medications and make a list of the names, monthly quantity, dosing instructions, and dosage with the name and phone number of the pharmacy where the medications were purchased. Also include the name of the doctor if different to the one you will be visiting.

o Add to your list any previous medications that either did not work or caused unusual symptoms. This list should include any antidepressants or mood-stabilizing medications. Note if the patient took these medications as prescribed or if they missed doses because this could cause a manic or depressed state if the patient has not complied with the doctor's orders.

o Make a list of symptoms, such as irritability, destructive tantrums, rage, bad mood, substance or

drug abuse, etc. It is also important to note how often these symptoms occur.
- o List any previous health problems (including past surgeries).

The next step is to think about why you are going to see the doctor and how to use the time effectively. Focus on the following to best communicate your needs and those of your loved one:

- o The appointment is to discuss the important issues you are about to face, such as your loved one's independence, needs, and treatments.
- o The appointment is not to discuss your own complaints.
- o Focus on the future. Focus on the best treatment options and ways to help them prepare for their future with bipolar disorder.

At the Doctor's Office
A doctor who is well versed in the treatment and diagnosis of mental disorders will ask you specific questions about the person and will be able to discuss disease care. If they are not expert, they can refer you to a physician familiar with bipolar disorder. They can also refer you to the resources you need, such as books and websites where you can learn more about what to expect when caring for the person with bipolar disorder.

The physician may do the following:

- o Ask about the person's common ADLs (activities of daily living), sleeping habits, medication compliance, and unusual behaviors.
- o Explain about diagnostic tests, such as laboratory studies, neurological tests, and an examination.

o Perform depression scale and mood or temperament scale tests to help with making a diagnosis and explain what to expect in the future.
o Schedule the next visit and let you know how often you should come back.

If you do not understand what the doctor is telling you or they are using medical jargon or words that you do not understand, ask them to explain it again. Using different (layperson's) words or drawing or showing you an illustration can help you to understand. Make sure to bring up anything that you want to discuss that the doctor may not have mentioned or discussed. Do not leave the office without understanding everything the doctor told you. Make sure you tell the doctor everything that you know about the individual's general health, including all symptoms and problems.

Doctors are often so focused on their patient load or the time allotted to each patient that they can be impatient or rushed and they may forget to talk about the disease, further diagnostic testing, or treatment options. If a misunderstanding arises during your appointment, promptly discuss it with the doctor.

Do not be afraid to ask specific questions. These questions are important for you to ask and have answered, and do not worry if you get home and realize that you have forgotten to ask some of your questions. Make another list and either fax or e-mail the questions with a request for an answer, call the doctor, or take them on your next visit. Here are some questions that you should ask if the doctor is suspecting a possible diagnosis of bipolar disorder:

o What does the diagnosis mean? Can you explain it in a way that I will understand?
o Should we seek a specialist?
o How many patients do you treat with bipolar disorder?

o What medications are available for bipolar disorder?
o What are the risks and benefits of the medications?
o Are there any treatments that work together or in conjunction with one another?
o What are the side effects?
o How long will they have to take this medicine?
o Should we consider participating in a drug trial?
o What are the risks and benefits?
o Under what circumstances should we call your office?
o What can we expect in the near future and over time?
o Do you have any written material on this disease? If not, who does?
o Are there any organizations or community services that can help?
o Is there anything that we can change at home to make things easier or safer?
o Is there anything else we should know?

When you are concluding your visit, do not forget to ask for referrals or recommendations for community support that can help you to prepare for the daily challenges of caregiving. As well, review what you have just learned with your friend or family member who accompanied you to the visit. Have the patient sign a medical record release so that you can communicate with the doctor about the patient. This is a critical document; without it, the doctor cannot communicate with you.

At the end of your visit to the doctor, you will know or have a good idea about the diagnosis. If the diagnosis is bipolar disorder, you may be upset or even angry as to why this has happened to you, your family, and friends. These are normal reactions, but you must put these feelings behind you. Take comfort in the fact that you now know the diagnosis, you know there are treatments available, and you can plan your life accordingly. The months or even years of uncertainty as to why your family member or friend was behaving the way they were are now over. Focus your energies on taking care of the person with bipolar disorder and learn how to handle the burden of being a caregiver. Most of all, learn how to take care of yourself in this new world that you are entering.

After the Visit to the Doctor's Office
It is a good idea to make a diary or mood chart of day-to-day activities and any changes that occur with the person affected. This will be helpful for subsequent visits to the doctor. Include the following:

- Changes in symptoms (mood, behavior) — When they started, frequency, time of day.
- How the prescribed treatments are working — What has improved; what has worsened?
- Any possible changes in mood, behavior, or activity since the start of new medications.
- Notes about their general health, such as fatigue, headaches, irritability, listlessness, etc.
- Notes about your own mental and physical health.
- Questions about additional help that you may need.

A simple way to keep this diary is to use a calendar to record the current mood. Ideally, both the patient and the caregiver would do this. Use a scale, such as +, 0, and −. If it has been a good day, place a + on the calendar. If it has been a really good day (almost too good?), place a ++ on that day. If it has been way too good, then place +++ on that day. You can use a similar scale for bad or − days. This becomes very valuable in helping to detect early changes or trends in moods that might require adjustments with medication.

The person with bipolar disorder creates many challenges for the caregiver and for the clinicians who treat them. Working together as a team will help to create a supportive environment that can provide a foundation for adequate and effective care, creating a better quality of life for the person living with bipolar disorder.

How Often Should I Talk with the Doctor?

During acute mania or depression, most people talk with their doctor at least once a week, or even every day, to monitor symptoms, medication doses, and side effects. As your patient recovers, they will see the doctor less often. When they are symptom free, they might see their doctor for a quick review every few months. Regardless of scheduled appointments or blood tests, call the doctor if they have:

o   Suicidal or violent feelings
o   Changes in mood, sleep, or energy
o   Changes in medication side effects
o   Need for over-the-counter medication (cold or pain medicine)
o   An acute medical illness or need for surgery, extensive dental care, or changes in other medicines they take
o   A change in their medical situation, such as pregnancy

3. Symptoms and Diagnosis

We have already noted that the diagnosis for bipolar disorder can be difficult, especially for the primary care provider who is not an expert in differentiating mood disorders and other diseases associated with the brain. If your doctor is not an expert, you must get a referral for a psychiatric evaluation. If the patient is a child or adolescent, make sure that you are referred to a physician experienced in diagnosing children. While the diagnosis of bipolar disorder can be very difficult in adults, it is much harder in children and they need the diagnosis of a medical specialist.

Nobody wants to go to their doctor when they are feeling good. When the bipolar person is feeling good, they may well be in a manic phase, deny their mania, and enjoy the experience in contrast to the depressive phase when they have trouble coping and feel bad about themselves. Consequently, the doctor usually sees the patient when they are depressed. The bipolar patient does not know what "normal" is until they have experienced it, usually as a result of medication.

In bipolar disorder, the many symptoms of depression and mania occur frequently, often daily, and last for weeks, months, or even years. However, some individuals may not have an episodic course on a regular basis; some patients will experience long periods without depression or mania. In some cases, such as in bipolar I disorder, the patient may have only experienced one episode of mania in their lifetime. Usually the patient shifts (cycles) from one pole to the other and, depending on the severity of the symptoms, their lives and the lives of those around them may be seriously disrupted if they are not diagnosed and treated correctly.

We cannot emphasize enough the importance of obtaining a correct diagnosis so that the correct course of treatment can be prescribed. The best chance of getting a correct diagnosis is to make sure that the patient sees a doctor experienced in mood disorders and preferably a psychiatrist. Remember that it may take more than one visit for the doctor to make the diagnosis. You may become frustrated waiting for the proper diagnosis. At the present time, it takes from 7–17 years (depending where in the bipolar spectrum the patient lies) to obtain an accurate diagnosis. There are no blood tests or other chemical or biochemical tests that will tell the doctor what diagnosis to make. The doctor must rely on family history, patient history, symptoms, observation, and some standardized questionnaires.

Collecting the Family History
Bipolar disorder runs in families; it is a hereditary disorder. If you suspect that a family member is showing symptoms that might be of a bipolar nature, start to write a family history. Write down the names of all the family members including parents, grandparents, great grandparents, aunts and uncles, etc. that you can remember. Add any comments you may have about their mental state, no matter how trivial it might seem, and include drug and alcohol abuse as well as any medical or psychiatric problems. When you have exhausted your own memory, contact other family members to see if they can support your memories and add to them. When you have finished, you will have a valuable document that you can give to the doctor, even if the diagnosis turns out to be completely negative for bipolar symptoms. If you do this in advance of your visit to the doctor, it will save time later.

The Family's Role in Diagnosis
While some individuals may recognize the symptoms themselves, it is often up to a family member to alert the

patient and then the physician, to make arrangements for a visit to the doctor's office, and to accompany the patient to the doctor's appointment. The family member can help to provide answers to the doctor's questions, such as:

o What symptoms have you noticed?
o When did the symptoms first appear?
o How have the symptoms changed over time?
o Does the person suffer from other medical conditions?
o Is the person taking medications? If so, what?
o Is there a family history of mood disorders, especially bipolar?
o Have you noticed personality changes, such as depression, irritability, mean-spiritedness, weeping, mood swings, etc.?
o Has there been a devastating event, such as the death of a spouse or close friend? Illness? Surgery? Have you noticed if they have become more distant, fatigued, or uninterested in socializing after the event?

Provide information to the doctor in as much detail as you can, even the embarrassing parts, because these can be very helpful to determine the severity of the symptoms. Were there any violent episodes against spouse, family, friends, or others; any arrests and what were they for; problems staying in employment; working 18-hour days; trouble getting out of bed; etc.? If the patient told you how they felt before, during, and after these events, it is all useful information for the doctor. Write everything down and organize the events and thoughts so that it will be more understandable for the doctor.

The Diagnosis of Bipolar Disorder
Any suggestion of mood disorders, especially diagnoses of bipolar disorder, in a family history should immediately make a physician, expert or not, consider that bipolar disorder is a possible diagnosis. If the patient presents with symptoms of episodic depression as well as a family history of bipolar

disorder, the physician should certainly consider bipolar disorder. Whereas mania is the diagnostic feature of bipolar disorder, the dominant symptom is depression.

As we noted in the previous chapter, when you go to the doctor, especially if it is for a first visit, you should collect and take the following information along with the family history:

- o A history of the symptoms that you and the patient have detected
- o The frequency of the symptoms
- o An estimate of the severity of the symptoms
- o A history of previous medications that the patient is no longer taking
- o A description of the patient's response to the medications they are no longer taking
- o A list of medications the patient is now taking, the dosage, and the frequency

All this information will give the doctor clues as to a possible diagnosis. In addition, if you suspect bipolar disorder yourself because you have been reading about the subject, do not be afraid to tell the doctor because if the doctor is not experienced in making this diagnosis, it may not have occurred to him.

For the physician or psychiatrist experienced with the DSM-IV diagnostic criteria (see below and Glossary), the diagnosis of bipolar I or bipolar II disorder may be relatively straightforward, particularly when major depressive episodes and manic or hypomanic episodes are obvious. The diagnosis of mixed state, cyclothymia, or bipolar NOS is usually much more difficult because the symptoms are harder to detect since they may be masked by comorbidities or the symptoms may not be severe enough to be readily noticed by the patient, caregiver, or doctor.

In coming to a diagnosis, the doctor must eliminate the other possible diagnoses and while mania or hypomania are the symptoms of only a few diseases (see below), depression is a symptom of many diseases and is a disease (unipolar depression) on its own. It is primarily in the realm of the depression pole that the diagnosis becomes confused and the patient may be misdiagnosed. Ruling out normal physiological depression apparent, for example, in some women during their menstrual cycle, the depression seen during substance abuse, as well as depression that is the symptom of comorbidity or even the side effects of medications, can be very difficult for the doctor or even the expert. The patient should receive a thorough medical exam with blood tests and other tests to help rule out other diagnoses.

Your doctor should use an interview process, a part of which should include one or more of the questionnaires described later in this chapter to help him come to a diagnosis. If the doctor has doubts, or if you have doubts about the given diagnosis, you must ask for a referral to a psychiatrist so a thorough psychiatric review can be conducted.

It is likely that your first visit to a doctor will be to the patient's primary care provider. They are responsible to diagnose and prescribe the correct treatment or refer you to a psychiatrist or other expert to diagnose the mental disorder. Unfortunately, statistics show that bipolar disorder is less well recognized and rarely contemplated when a patient presents with depressive features to a primary care provider. The likelihood that they will diagnose bipolar disorder correctly is not high. To further complicate the picture, the majority of patients who go to their doctor for a suspected mental condition display medical and psychiatric symptoms, both of which will have to be treated. Very many patients have never had a full-blown manic episode, a symptom of bipolar I disorder. They may well have had hypomanic episodes (bipolar II or cyclothymia, depending on the severity of the depressive phases), but these can be very difficult to detect, and even the patient and family members may be uncertain if hypomanic episodes have occurred.

Bipolar disorder is easily confused with ADHD, unipolar depression, or depression resulting as a symptom of another illness, and the nonexpert physician will not always make the correct diagnosis. If you are uncertain about the diagnosis you have received, insist on a referral and then check the credentials of the doctor to whom you are referred to make sure they have the necessary experience and knowledge.

Once again, we cannot emphasize enough the need for the correct diagnosis because the consequences of a wrong diagnosis are serious. The bipolar person is much more functionally impaired and has a higher risk of suicide or self-harm than patients with unipolar depression and other mood disorders. While antidepressants work well in the depressed patient, bipolar patients require a mood stabilizer (see Chapter 5) in addition to the antidepressant. The choice of medication is further complicated by where in the bipolar spectrum the patient is diagnosed. Are they bipolar I, bipolar II, cyclothymic, or bipolar NOS?

The doctor or psychiatrist will come to a conclusion on a diagnosis based on the symptoms that they see or that the patient or you, the caregiver, have provided. As we noted previously, it may take several visits for the doctor to come to a diagnosis. The American Psychiatric Association has compiled a set of diagnostic criteria to describe many mental disorders including bipolar, depression, mania and hypomania, etc. These criteria are referred to as the "Diagnostic and Statistical Manual of Mental Disorders (DSM-IV)". You may well hear about or read about DSM-IV because the use of this acronym is quite common in the medical literature. Later in this chapter, we list some of the common symptoms of these disorders and we provide the information to compare bipolar disorder with unipolar depression to better illustrate how these disorders are different and, therefore, why they have to be treated differently. However, first we will consider and describe the possible diagnoses.

By no means is there agreement between psychiatrists and other knowledgeable doctors about the bipolar spectrum and how to diagnose bipolar disorder. Some doctors believe that bipolar disorder is overdiagnosed and some believe it is underdiagnosed; some recognize the full bipolar spectrum and others do not. What we present in this chapter is our view on the diagnosis of bipolar disorder.

<u>What Tests are Available?</u>
There are some written questionnaires available that help in the diagnosis of bipolar disorder. It is a good idea for both the patient and the caregiver to complete the questionnaire based on how they each see the mood and behavioral changes in the patient. You can take completed questionnaires to your doctor on your first visit.

Mood Disorder Questionnaire (MDQ)
This questionnaire was developed by Dr. Robert Hirschfeld to help the doctor or psychiatrist determine what kind of mood disorder the patient is experiencing. It is in common use and can be downloaded from many Internet sites. Try www.bipolar.com. Because this questionnaire provides only yes or no answers, it can provide an accurate diagnosis, but it can also be wrong depending on how the patient and caregiver answer the questions. We recommend using both the MDQ and the Bipolar Spectrum Diagnostic Scale (see below) to give a better picture of the symptoms.

Bipolar Spectrum Diagnostic Scale (BSDS)
The BSDS was developed by Dr. Ronald Pies to help doctors better diagnose bipolar states. It is particularly sensitive to the detection of bipolar II disorder. Because this scale does not

give yes and no answers, it does not make a diagnosis, but it does provide the doctor with much of the information that will help them to make an accurate diagnosis. The BSDS can also be found on many Internet sites. Try looking at this one: http://www.nelmh.org/page_view.asp?c=3&did=2819&fc=00 2002007.

Goldberg Mood (Mania and Depression) Scales
The Goldberg Mood Scales were developed by Dr. Ivan Goldberg and are not intended for use in making a diagnosis. These scales are designed to measure changes in the severity of depression and mania that result from psychotherapeutic or psychopharmacologic treatment. There are two separate scales, one for depression and one for mania. If your patient is already taking medications for their mood disorder, these scales will measure changes in the patient's behavior and will provide an indication of when the patient should visit their doctor as symptoms change. The Goldenberg Mood Scales can also be found on the Internet. Try looking at this site: http://home.blarg.net/~charlatn/depression/scales.txt.

TEMPS-A (Temperament Evaluation of Memphis, Pisa, Paris, and San Diego Autoquestionnaire)
The TEMPS-A questionnaire is designed to measure temperament variations and is increasingly used to help diagnose bipolar disorder. The questionnaire is completed by the patient and asks 110 true or false questions about how they have viewed themselves for most of their life (see the references at the end of the chapter for more information).

What are the Episodes in the Bipolar Spectrum?
When describing the symptoms of a bipolar person, we talk about them having "episodes". An episode is nothing more than an occurrence or recurrence of one of the symptoms of bipolar disorder. However, to describe the symptoms of the disorders in the bipolar spectrum adequately, it is useful to break them down into their episodes, such as:

- o Major depressive episode
- o Manic episode
- o Mixed episode (both manic and depressive episodes occur at the same time)
- o Hypomanic episode

We will discuss comorbidities and other complications of diagnosis later in this chapter, but one of the considerations when discussing the symptoms of these episodes in the bipolar spectrum is to be aware that the symptoms are not being caused by something else, such as drug or alcohol abuse, another medical condition, or another mental disorder that has been diagnosed.

<u>What are the Symptoms of a Major Depressive Episode?</u>
When at least five of the symptoms listed below have been present during the same 2-week period and represent a change from previous mood and behavior patterns, and at least one of the symptoms is either (1) depressed mood or (2) loss of interest or pleasure, the patient may be experiencing a major depressive episode.

The symptoms may be recognized by the patient or by the caregiver and occur every day or almost every day and cannot be related to an obvious cause, such as the death of a loved one. Also, the symptoms cause significant impairment in the patient's ability to function at school, work, socially, or at home.

- o Depressed mood most of the day (sadness, helplessness, tearful). In children (see section on diagnosis in children later in this chapter) and adolescents, the depressed mood may appear as irritability.
- o Markedly diminished interest or pleasure in most or all of their activities most of the day.

- o Significant, unanticipated weight loss or weight gain (a change of more than 5% of body weight in a month), or decrease or increase in appetite.
- o Disturbed sleep pattern. Insomnia (unable to sleep) or hypersomnia (excessive sleep with inability to stay awake).
- o Purposeless motion, such as pacing the same path, hand wringing, taking clothes off and putting them back on, etc. The purposeless motion usually originates in a mental tension. This is called psychomotor agitation.
- o Slowing of thought processes and reduced physical movement that may be accompanied by psychosis. This is called psychomotor retardation or motormental retardation.
- o Loss of energy, fatigue.
- o Feelings of worthlessness.
- o Feelings of inappropriate guilt.
- o Unable to concentrate, reduced ability to think or reason.
- o Indecisive.
- o Suicidal thoughts or specific plans to commit suicide or actual attempt at suicide.
- o Thoughts about death.

What are the Symptoms of a Manic Episode?

Often the person feels normal when they have a manic episode and do not recognize it. They feel good and there is denial about being manic.

For a set of symptoms to be considered a manic episode, they must last a minimum of 1 week or of any duration if the symptoms are severe enough to cause hospitalization. The key characteristics are an abnormally and persistently elevated expansive or irritable mood in which at least three of the following symptoms are significantly present and persist throughout the manic episode. If the elevated mood is only irritability, then four of the following symptoms are required for the diagnosis. The symptoms are of sufficient severity that they cause marked impairment in the patient's ability to function at school, work, socially, or at home. The symptoms may be severe enough to require hospitalization to prevent the patient from harming himself or others, and there may also be evidence of psychosis.

o   Inflated self-esteem or grandiosity
o   Reduced need for sleep, 3 hours a night is enough
o   Talkative and feels the need to keep on talking
o   Racing thoughts
o   Easily distracted
o   Increased goal-directed activity
o   Psychomotor agitation (see above or Glossary)
o   Excessive involvement in high-risk, pleasurable activities, such as shopping sprees, sexual conquests, unwise investments

What are Symptoms of a Hypomanic Episode?
The symptoms and requirements for the diagnosis of a hypomanic episode are the same as for a manic episode except that they last for a shorter period of time (at least 4 days compared to at least 1 week for a manic episode). The symptoms may be less severe than in a manic episode, but there is nevertheless a marked change in functioning in the patient when compared to their "normal" state that is readily recognized by family members and friends. The patient will be able to function at school, work, and social settings. The symptoms will not be severe enough to require hospitalization and there will be no evidence of psychosis.

What are the Symptoms of a Mixed Episode?
Once we know the symptoms of a major depressive episode and a manic episode, we know the criteria for a mixed episode because a mixed episode occurs when the manic episode and the major depressive episode exist at the same time. For the

mixed episode to be diagnosed, the symptoms should last for at least a 1-week period and occur almost every day. Also, the symptoms are of sufficient severity that they cause marked impairment in the patient's ability to function at school, work, socially, or at home. The symptoms may be severe enough to require hospitalization to prevent the patient from harming himself or others, and there may also be evidence of psychosis.

Mixed states are found in bipolar I, bipolar II, and bipolar spectrum disorders. They are more common in women and are often associated with thyroid abnormalities and failure to respond to lithium (the standard treatment for bipolar I disorder).

The diagnosis for mixed states is very difficult for the doctor to make and it often occurs after the patient's symptoms have been made worse by antidepressant therapy or when they fail to respond to other treatments and become hospitalized.

What are the Symptoms of Disorders in the Bipolar Spectrum?
Now that we have an idea of what constitutes the symptoms of the episodes described above, we can identify the diagnostic criteria for the main disorders in the bipolar spectrum:

o Bipolar I — Severe depression with at least one episode of mania.
o Bipolar II — Severe depression with separate phases of hypomania.
o Cyclothymia — Mild depression with separate hypomanic phases.
o Bipolar disorder NOS (not otherwise specified) — Bipolar features exist, but the diagnosis fits no other category.
o Mixed states — Combined presence of full manic and full depressive symptoms at the same time.
o Bipolar spectrum disorder — This disorder has been proposed to be part of the bipolar spectrum even

though no manic or hypomanic episode is detected. It is recognized by the patient's failure to respond to antidepressants.

Diagnosing Bipolar Disorder in Children and Adolescents (Early Onset Bipolar)

The criteria (as described in the DSM-IV) for the diagnosis of bipolar disorder in children are the same as for adults at the present time, although it is clear that the symptoms in children and adolescents can be quite different. In the remainder of this section, we provide you with some guidelines as to what you might watch for so you can pass this information to the child's or adolescent's doctor. There are no statistics on the prevalence of bipolar disorder in the child and adolescent population, but many may have early onset bipolar disorder, perhaps as much as one-third of the 3.4 million diagnosed with depression.

The first thing you will notice is that the child's mood and behavior are not "normal". You will know this because of the comparisons you make with siblings and other children. The child is different and, therefore, their symptoms require closer scrutiny. It is time to let the family doctor know that you suspect something is wrong.

We cannot emphasize enough to you that you must see the doctor and explain the symptoms as best you are able so you can receive the correct diagnosis for the child. Early intervention with medication and therapy will give the child the best hope for coping with the disease. All too often, the diagnosis is not made until years after symptoms are first seen. The symptoms get worse over time and the child is less able to cope in school, at home, and in their social world. Serious consequences can ensue, such as expulsion from school, drug abuse, attempted or actual suicide, or the development of personality disorders.

When you take the child to the doctor, you should not expect an immediate diagnosis. The diagnosis of bipolar disorder is very difficult in children and their disease is often masked by or occurs with other disorders, such as depression, conduct disorder, ADHD, oppositional-defiant disorder, panic disorder, obsessive-compulsive disorder, and others. In adolescents, bipolar disorder may be misdiagnosed as borderline personality disorder, schizophrenia, or post-traumatic stress disorder.

As you can see, it is difficult for the doctor to make the diagnosis and it is essential that you be referred to an expert in child mental illnesses to give the child the best chance for an accurate diagnosis so they can start therapy as soon as possible. If the child receives the wrong diagnosis, their symptoms may actually be made worse by receiving the wrong medication.

It is very important to the doctor that you tell them of any family history of mental disorders because bipolar disorder is a hereditary disorder.

<u>What are the Symptoms of Early Onset Bipolar Disorder?</u>
Symptoms of bipolar disorder have been found in infants (clingy, tantrums or rages, difficult to settle, erratic sleep) so there is no lower limit on the age at which bipolar disorder might be diagnosed. It is never too early to go to the doctor when you see any of the symptoms.

Many children will have mood and energy shifts several times a day resulting in chronic irritability in the child. These rapid cycling periods are commonly observed in children with bipolar disorder and the child may have a few periods of wellness between the cycles. Destructive tantrums that can last for hours, especially if the child is older than 4 years, and any indication that the child wants to hurt or even kill themselves are also very common and definitely a sign that the child should visit the doctor.

One of the problems of recognizing the symptoms in children is that they *are* children and they exhibit many behaviors that are not acceptable in adults. It is important to differentiate symptoms of bipolar disorder or other illness from what you see in other "normal" children.

Some of the common symptoms of bipolar disorder in children include destructive temper tantrums, failure to make expected weight gains, marked irritability, frequent mood swings lasting a few hours to a few days, defiance, hyperactivity, separation anxiety, lack of interest in play, social anxiety, "silly" behavior, carbohydrate or sweet cravings, as well as the symptoms you will find in adults (see above). Depending on the age of the child, you may also find bed-wetting (especially boys), hypersexuality, daydreaming, motor and vocal tics, manipulative behavior, learning disability, lying, and poor short-term memory. As the caregiver, you should watch out for any symptoms that you consider as significant and that you consider as "not normal" behavior. Write them down and give them to the doctor when you visit.

Bipolar Disorder in Adolescents

As a caregiver, you must be vigilant. Statistics show that, on average, it takes 10 years between the time symptoms first appear and the time correct treatment begins. Think how much damage has been done to the adolescent and the family during that time.

The symptoms of bipolar disorder in adolescents are similar to those seen in adults. Puberty is a time of major physical and mental change in boys and girls. It is a time of risk, anxiety, self-awareness, and confusion, and almost any traumatic event can trigger a first depressive or manic episode. In girls, there is the onset of menses that can trigger the disorder and the severity of symptoms may vary within the menstrual cycle.

If four or more of the symptoms described above for mania, hypomania, or depression persist for more than 2 weeks, you should take the adolescent to the doctor for evaluation. Early intervention and the correct diagnosis and treatment will make a big difference in the quality of life for the adolescent during these crucially important years of their development. It will also make the lives of the caregiver, family, and friends a whole lot easier if the adolescent receives the correct treatment.

Drug and alcohol abuse is common in adolescents. The easy availability of mind-altering substances, such as alcohol, marijuana, cocaine, amphetamines, ecstacy, and other drugs, and the pleasure derived from the use of these drugs, make them attractive to the adolescent. However, substance abuse is a common symptom of bipolar disorder and any adolescent who abuses these substances should be taken to their doctor to be evaluated for a mood disorder.

If the adolescent has already been diagnosed with bipolar disorder, you should be aware that substance abuse is a symptom of the disorder and you should seek medical attention as soon as you see indications that the adolescent is abusing alcohol or drugs. If addiction does occur, it is important to treat both the addiction and the bipolar disorder at the same time.

Misdiagnosis – the Reasons and the Consequences?
Bipolar disorder is difficult to diagnose in most cases and, unfortunately, is commonly misdiagnosed. There may be underlying conditions that are causing the symptoms of mania or depression that confuse the diagnosis, or all the symptoms of bipolar disorder are not readily apparent and the patient is misdiagnosed with a similar disorder, such as unipolar

depression or ADHD. It may also be that the physician is insufficiently skilled to make the correct diagnosis.

Depression is a far more common symptom of other disease states than is mania. For example, mania is found as a symptom only in bipolar disorder, lupus, and psychosis, whereas depression is found as a symptom of many diseases, such as Alzheimer's, Huntington's, Addison's, hypothyroidism, thyroid disorders, lupus, and many more. Depression may also be a symptom of physiological functions, such as stress, menopause, premenstrual syndrome, and postpartum depression, and may also be a symptom of substance abuse, such as cannabis, amphetamines, or cocaine.

The Role of Comorbidity in Misdiagnosis
It is not difficult to imagine that if a person is suffering from more than one illness, the diagnosis of any of the illnesses will be more difficult. This is the problem with comorbid illnesses and bipolar disorder. Estimates indicate that 50% or more of the patients with bipolar disorder have medical or psychiatric comorbid illnesses. Not only does the comorbid illness complicate an already difficult diagnosis, but it may also complicate the treatment.

Certain conditions are particularly problematic when they are comorbid with bipolar disorder. These conditions include thyroid (hyperthyroid or hypothyroid) disorders, drug and alcohol abuse, ADHD, borderline personality disorder, and other personality disorders.

Consequences of Nondiagnosis
If you have read this far and have determined that your family member or friend does not have any of the symptoms of bipolar disorder, you will probably not seek a diagnosis, although you might still want to look up some of the Internet sites that we list at the end of this chapter to inform yourself

more about the disease and related diseases. After all, you did get as far as reading this book.

If you are uncertain about anything here, we encourage you to visit a doctor to obtain a diagnosis if there is one. The consequences of not receiving a diagnosis are serious if the person turns out to be diagnosed with bipolar disorder eventually. Their symptoms will worsen; they will be less able or unable to cope with school, work, family, and social life; they may do harm to themselves and others; and they may even succeed at suicide. The consequences for the undiagnosed and untreated person with bipolar disorder stretch beyond the person afflicted to family members and friends who must find a way to deal with the problems. Many will turn away and the person will be left with nobody who understands what is wrong with them.

No excuses: make the time and make the doctor make the time.

After the Diagnosis
Once the diagnosis has been made, the physician may or may not develop a health care plan for the person with bipolar disorder that will strive to:

- o Maximize functioning and independence
- o Foster a safe and secure environment
- o Start medication
- o Find a support group and other groups that can help the caregiver

Patient surveillance and health maintenance visits will be scheduled every 3–6 months to:

- o Monitor cognition and behavior with testing
- o Address and treat comorbid conditions
- o Evaluate ongoing medications

- o Check for sleep disturbances
- o Establish programs to improve behavior and mood
- o Work closely with family and caregivers
- o Encourage modulation of the patient's environment

If the physician does not provide you with a health care plan, ask them to do so. If you are unable to discuss this with the doctor at the time of diagnosis, you can make a new appointment to discuss the health care plan specifically. The plan will include the need for medication and counseling that will involve one or more doctors, such as a psychiatrist and a licensed therapist.

Now that the diagnosis has been made and you have the plan of care, it is time to start planning and making the decisions that will influence the next few years of your life. You have to plan for your life as a caregiver and you have to plan to take care of yourself while you are fulfilling the caregiver role.

After the diagnosis of bipolar disorder has been made, you are now fully involved in the disease and involved in taking care of your patient. They will need your help, your support, and they need you to take care of them.

Internet Resources
http://www.dbsalliance.org/info/bipolar.html
http://psychcentral.com/disorders/sx20.htm
http://www.nmha.org/bipolar/public/signs.cfm
http://www.bipolarhome.org/
http://www.nlm.nih.gov/medlineplus/bipolardisorder.html
http://www.ncpamd.com/Bipolar.htm
http://bipolar.about.com/cs/menu_diagnosis/a/0401_how_diag
.htm
http://www.helpguide.org/mental/bipolar_disorder_symptoms
_treatment.htm

References

1. Akiskal HS, Akiskal KK, Haykal RF, Manning JS, Connor PD: TEMPS-A: progress towards validation of a self-rated clinical version of the Temperament Evaluation of the Memphis, Pisa, Paris, and San Diego Autoquestionnaire. J Affect Disord 2005, 85: 3–16.
2. Akiskal HS, Mendlowicz MV, Girardin J-L, Rapaport MH, Kelsoe JR, Gillin JC, Smith TL: TEMPS-A: validation of a short version of a self-rated instrument designed to measure variations in temperament. J Affect Disord 2005, 85: 45–52.

4. Time for Planning

Now that bipolar disorder has been diagnosed, it is time to make some decisions and start planning for the future. The role of the caregiver will be totally consuming and it is essential that the caregiver plan to take care of themselves as well as the patient. Do not forget yourself — you, the caregiver! Burnout can creep up out of the blue if you do not take care of yourself and plan for your own well-being.

The first crucial decision is to decide who will be the primary caregiver. Frequently, this will be the spouse or parent, but if no spouse or parent is available or if the spouse or parent is unable to cope with the responsibilities of being a caregiver to a bipolar patient, then an alternative caregiver will be needed, either a family member or, perhaps, a friend. You may decide to consult your physician to obtain a medical opinion as to your suitability to serve as a caregiver.

Frequently, of course, there is no choice. You are the spouse or parent and nobody else is stepping forward. You do not feel that you can abandon your loved one and so, like it or not, you are *it*. Make the most of it. Learn to enjoy the good times together and plan carefully to make sure that you can do the very best for you both.

Whoever the caregiver is, they will need to build their own support group from family members, friends, and external groups. More of this later.

Bipolar disorder is a lifelong disease. Those with the severest form will need care and attention until they die and you must plan to make sure that care is available to them. From what you have read already, you know that the average life expectancy for the person with bipolar disorder is 7–8 years less than the national average of around 80 years. Women live 6–7 years longer than men and your planning should take this into account. Do not forget that with medical advances, life expectancy is increasing all the time. So without making the planning process too complex, we have prepared some guidelines to help you.

One of the first significant issues you will have to deal with is the episodic manifestation of the symptoms of depression and mania. Since you will not know precisely when the episodes will start or end, you must be prepared to deal with them at all times. This will place an extra burden on you so you must determine if you are able to cope alone, through good planning and organization, or if you will need the help of a family member or friend. If none are available, find out what outside resources are available to you.

There will be times when urgent or emergency action will be needed as the patient dives into an episode. At these times, you will implement a crisis-prevention and intervention plan, the details of which are described in Chapter 7.

What is the point of planning? Planning helps to take out the uncertainty about the future. Planning makes you do your homework so that you will be able to identify potential problem areas and solve them in a timely manner. Planning helps you to gather the information you need so that you make the best decisions for the person with bipolar disorder and for yourself.

Depending on the severity of the symptoms and the amount of care needed by your patient, you will have to decide if they will require constant supervision, making caregiving a full-time job. Since 35% of all caregivers work outside the home, it becomes necessary to arrange either for professional care or for the caregiver to stop working and stay with the patient. In either case, the costs are considerable and planning for this eventuality is essential.

There are many practical issues for which you will have to plan including financial, legal, safety, etc. One of the most important for you, the caregiver, is time. Planning your time can make the difference between coping and not coping. Setting routine for the patient, while ensuring that you have time for yourself, is essential for you to lead a decent life.

For most people, financial planning will be a key concern and an area on which to focus. Some of the bipolar symptoms are shopping sprees, poor business decisions, and financial mismanagement leading to possible bankruptcy. You must protect the family finances by controlling your patient's access to bank accounts, credit and debit cards, and any other sources.

You should discuss with their doctor the likely outcome for your loved one.

- o Will care outside the home be required?
- o What kind of care will be required?
- o What is the probable cost of care?

However, there are other matters that require planning and the caregiver's attention, such as legal matters, therapy, moving, and contingency planning. What happens if something happens to you, the caregiver? Who will take your place?

We know that the individual's symptoms will get worse with time and they will become more dependent on the caregiver to the point that they may be totally dependent. As soon as the diagnosis is known, start the planning process to optimize available treatments and services, and to ease the burden on you.

Once again, we emphasize the importance of an early diagnosis. While the patient can make their wishes known, involve them as much as possible in the planning process. If you are not the one who paid the bills, arranged the finances, or took care of legal matters, you will have to learn these things and it will be much easier for you if the patient is able to participate.

As part of the planning process, you should start by educating yourself about bipolar disorder. Learn what happens as the disease progresses and learn how to deal with the patient in an effective manner. Remember that the patient is not going to be in control of what they do; the disease will take over their ability to control their moods and behaviors. As the caregiver, you are the one who must change to meet the patient's needs. Your communication style, attitudes, and ability to fill the patient's needs will be reflected in the well-being and behavior of the patient. There are many websites that can provide information on bipolar disorder and the bipolar spectrum, and we list some of these later in this book. Also, there are local and national associations that provide useful information and support for caregivers. This book will give you some of the guidance you need.

Financial and legal issues will play an important part in caring for the bipolar patient and these issues should be tended to immediately. Discuss as much as possible with your loved one when they are well enough to help you. If your family has an accountant, lawyer, financial planner, or other professional that has assisted you previously, identify them and locate their respective files and records. You should then contact each of these professionals to apprise them of the patient's condition and seek their advice. If you think it necessary, perhaps because your home records are incomplete or if you are not sure if they are complete, arrange to meet with the professionals so that you can become fully informed of the relevant financial and legal issues. It is not uncommon for spouses not to know of their financial status. They have been happy to leave financial and legal matters to their partner. This has to change. The caregiver must now be the person that is fully informed and starting to make the decisions on these critical issues.

If financial and legal professionals have not been involved with the patient's affairs, you must decide on your own ability to take on the responsibility of managing the household finances and any legal issues. If you do not feel sufficiently knowledgeable to take this on, talk to family members, maybe they can help. If you want professional help, ask for recommendations from friends who have had positive experiences with particular accountants, lawyers, and others.

You know that the person with bipolar disorder will cycle through stages of the disease and will probably decline over the years. Eventually, they will probably die from another disease. There are certain items that are very important to have in place so that there is no ambiguity about what to do in the late stages and after the death of the patient. Preferably, these legal documents should be drawn up while the patient is competent to have a say in the way their affairs will be handled, particularly the way they want to be treated when they are no longer in control of their moods and behavior. If you do not have these legal documents already in place, we recommend that you visit an attorney, either your family attorney or an attorney experienced in medical affairs, at the earliest opportunity.

The key documents to consider having in place are a will, medical and durable power of attorney, living will, health care surrogate, conservator, and do not resuscitate (DNR) order. Discuss these documents with your attorney to determine which are most appropriate for you and for the state in which you live.

These documents will establish your ability to make financial, legal, and medical decisions for the person with bipolar disorder when they are unable to make rational or calculated decisions themselves. There are distinct differences between each of these documents, all of which should be prepared with the assistance of an attorney.

- o A durable power of attorney (or POA) is a legal document that authorizes you, the caregiver, to either have financial power of attorney, health care power of attorney, or both, depending on how it is written. If you have both, a POA will allow you the ability to make all legal, health (treatment), caregiving, and financial decisions on behalf of the person with bipolar disorder.
- o The surrogate becomes the attorney-in-fact, and any competent adult can be selected to be the surrogate, although a member of the medical team should not be selected because of possible conflicts of interest. Select just one person to be the surrogate, although others may be selected to serve as alternates in the event the chosen person is unavailable or unable to make decisions. Surrogates cannot be held liable for decisions made regarding the patient's care or for costs associated with medical care. The surrogate can only make decisions when the patient is temporarily or permanently unable to make their own health care decisions.
- o A conservator handles all the legal oversight and decisions for health care in the person's best interest and is appointed by the court. A conservator can be a professional conservator (third party) or they can be a friend or family member who seeks conservatorship from the court.

- A living will establishes the wants and desires of the individual who authors the document. This may establish the health issues of the person and may include a DNR order.
- A DNR establishes the wishes that a person not have CPR performed in case of a heart attack or other accident or condition that may require CPR.
- A will establishes all of the wishes of an individual, which may include designating a POA in case of incapacitation, will include dispersement of assets, and could possibly contain the living will.

The next key issue is financial. It is vital that you identify and plan how to manage financial resources to recognize how monies should be spent and where there might be insufficient funds. The caregiver may be responsible for paying bills, arranging for benefit claims, investment decisions, tax returns, etc.

The first step is to locate and identify financial and insurance documents, such as insurance policies (life, long-term care, disability, health, auto, homeowner's), investments, bank accounts, pension and other retirement benefits, Social Security payments, other forms of income, deeds or mortgage papers, or ownership statements and bills. If you are uncertain what to do and your loved one cannot help, involve a family member who is more familiar with taking care of the financial responsibilities in their own household. You will quickly learn to take care of the details and make the decisions yourself. It is essential that you make sure that you have access to all the funds of the patient. If you are the spouse and you did not have joint bank accounts, joint investments, etc., you must make sure that the accounts are changed so that you have access to the funds. Do this while the patient is competent so that you do not have to go through more complicated and possibly costly procedures later.

Once you have determined that you have access to all the funds and insurance policies, you can start to make some calculations for what your income and expenses are going to be. Do not forget the equity that you may have in your home that can be turned into cash through loans, lines of credit, or a reverse mortgage.

Keep in mind that if you, the caregiver, are currently working and earning, you may eventually have to give up your job to take care of the patient or pay for someone else to do it, unless there is another family member or friend who can care for the patient without pay while you are at work. Do not underestimate the burden on yourself as you will have to decide if you are able to both work and take care of the patient when you come home.

Once you have an overview of the financial situation, you will be able to make a determination if there are sufficient financial resources to cover the cost of care. If you find there are sufficient funds available, you want to make sure that your financial resources are protected. This is probably not the time for you to invest in high-risk ventures, but look for a more conservative approach that will protect your capital and give you an acceptable level of return on your investments. A financial advisor can help you if you are not comfortable making these kinds of decisions.

If you find that you will not have the financial resources to take care of the patient or if you believe it will be very tight, you should start to look for other sources of financial support. Do you have any funds not already included in your calculations? Approach family members with your appraisal of the financial situation and get their input as to ways to help out. Can they contribute? How much can they contribute? Are there friends that were close enough to you or your loved one that might want to help?

To help you to obtain a realistic estimate of the cost of long-term care, it is a good idea to call several adult day care facilities and local specialist facilities for the mentally ill to find out their costs and what their projections are for cost increases. This knowledge will help you to project the cost of the last few years of the patient's life more accurately. Even though you may now say that you will never put your loved one in a mental health facility or other facility, the burden on the caregiver is a heavy one and you may no longer be able to cope after several years of caring.

Now what about you? What will happen to the patient if something happens to you and you are no longer able to take care of them? Make contingency plans and look into taking out (more) insurance on yourself to provide a financial safety net for yourself and those dependent on your income. Disability and life insurance should be considered, but talk to an insurance agent or a financial planner to see what may be best in your particular situation. As well, you should consider looking into long-term health care insurance to help cover costs of long-term care, both in the home and in a facility.

Find out if there is a family member or friend who will take over the role of caregiver if something should happen to you. If there is, make sure that you put the necessary legal documents in place to give them access to your assets and that they are named as caregiver/guardian. Consult an attorney about this. Remember... you could be in an accident tomorrow and you must make sure that you and your loved one are taken care of.

Budgeting
Knowing how much money is coming in (income) whether from jobs, investments, or other sources and knowing how much money is being spent (expenses) in the patient's household is essential for most people. Keep good records and prepare a budget for yourself. There are several good

computer programs around that do this in a very structured way, but if you prefer pen and paper, keep track of the items of expense and income so you always know what your financial situation is and, just as important, you make it possible for someone else to find out the financial situation if anything happens to you.

When budgeting, take into account what insurance benefits the patient may have. Are they eligible for Medicare or Medicaid? If so, is there Medigap insurance in place and, if not, does it make financial sense to get Medigap insurance? Does the patient have disability insurance that comes into effect? Is there long-term care insurance? Is there life insurance that could be used to provide cash? Are there any other retirement plans? What Social Security benefits does the patient receive? Is the patient eligible for Social Security disability income, supplemental security income, veteran's benefits, or any tax benefits? You may be eligible for medical expense deductions and dependent care credits on your tax return.

If the patient is still able to work, what employee benefits are available and if they become unemployed by no fault of their own or if they retire from their employer, what benefits will continue?

More Planning
Now that you have taken care of financial and legal matters, you should turn your attention to planning your daily life and that of the patient. Your life as the caregiver will change; there is no doubt about that. If you plan your days and live a more structured life than you may otherwise have done, you will also be able to plan for yourself, for the time you will need for yourself.

The person with bipolar disorder needs help. As the disease gets worse, the patient needs more help. This is the way it is.

You must establish routines for them and for yourself to minimize stress on you both.

Recognizing what help they need will help you to plan your days. As their condition changes, you may have to change your daily plans to accommodate those changes. Remember that it is you who must change; they are not capable of changing to accommodate your needs. They are dependent on you to guide and care for them.

As a start, identify their needs and make the time available to take care of each one. They may need help dressing, seeing to personal care (particularly hygiene), doing chores, making meals, meeting friends, or going out. Your role in their activities is to give support, encouragement, help when needed, and supervision. You should be aware of their limitations and encourage them to do things at which they are able to succeed and enjoy. Keep things simple and be patient with them so that they are able to enjoy what they are doing. Remember that this is about them and not about you.

The less stress the better. Be aware that what may not be stressful to you may be stressful to the patient, and you must keep this in mind when planning an outing. Planning activities for the patient is also beneficial for the caregiver. You know where the patient is so you do not have to worry about them. You can see them having fun and participating with friends, other patients, or you. Being assured as to their safety and well-being helps to reduce your own stress.

Safety
Depending on the severity of the bipolar disorder, immediate surroundings can become a dangerous place if precautions are not taken. Remember that the patient is capable of self-harm and suicide, and is capable of harming others. It is time to look at the patient's residence and make safe anything that could be

considered dangerous or might even be used as a weapon. More guidance on safety matters is provided in Chapter 6.

Planning for the End
While this can be a difficult topic to discuss, there should be no doubt in the minds of the caregiver and family members that the patient will die, directly or indirectly, as a result of bipolar disorder. Eventually, you will have to assume full responsibility for the loved one's affairs.

Encourage the patient, as soon as possible after diagnosis, to select an advance directive (either a living will or a durable POA) that expresses their wishes for treatment at the end of their life. It is important to use the advance directive form(s) recognized by the state in which care will be provided. If no advance directive is drawn up, it may be advisable to consult an attorney for advice on how to proceed, as there are other options (such as conservatorship) that may better serve the patient.

Become familiar with the range of medical care available:

o Treatment strategies
o Aggressive care
o Feeding tubes and IV hydration
o Conservative care
o Palliative care (end of life)

Be prepared to make decisions.

o Be guided by the person's wishes and preferences
o Work with family members and the health care team
o Consider using a trusted third party to facilitate the decision-making process

Resolving Family Conflicts

Be prepared for family conflicts. There may well be opinions from family members about how to manage the end of the person's life, even when there are legal documents in place that describe the person's wishes. Make sure that you have the legal documents in place that make it clear who has the decision-making responsibility. If the conflict becomes unmanageable for you, consider involving a third party who understands the law and the person's wishes, and can help to defuse a difficult situation.

After Death

When the patient eventually dies, many caregivers feel a great sense of relief. The burden of caregiving is over. Do not feel guilty about having this reaction as it is very common and understandable. Your own normal life can now resume without the need to care for another, and you may find that your health improves, particularly if you have been depressed. There are many reports of caregivers who experience rapid recovery from depression after the death of the person they have been caring for.

Planning for You

Your role of caregiver will be demanding and there will be times when you feel that you cannot cope. In Chapter 6, we present some tips and tools for caregivers that we believe will help you in your daily life as a caregiver. It will help you if you structure your life and plan your day so there is time for you to pursue what you enjoy, whether it is reading, meeting friends, watching television, hobbies, or whatever else can help you to relax and enjoy your own life. Find out what resources are available in your community. There are options available to help both you and the patient. Consider attending a support group and learn how to care for yourself as a caregiver. A stressed, overtired caregiver cannot provide the type of care they are trying so hard to give.

If you decide to continue working after the person has been diagnosed with bipolar disorder, you will have to plan for day care with family, friends, or with a day care facility. Your time with the bipolar patient will then be planned around your work schedule. Even though you will have just a few hours to work with, make sure that you establish the routine for the individual and make sure that you plan some time for yourself.

5. Therapies

There is no cure for bipolar disorder at the present time. Therapies focus on alleviating the symptoms of the disease so the patients can manage their daily lives. The good news is that the therapies work as long as patients follow the treatment plans provided by their doctors and therapists. Different doctors have different ideas about treatment plans for bipolar patients so do not be surprised if what we write here is not what your doctor does. It does not mean that we are wrong or that he or she is wrong. The doctor will prescribe treatment based on experience, while we are giving a general view of the more commonly prescribed treatments.

Effective therapies for bipolar disorder usually include the combination of medications and psychotherapy. In this chapter, we will present the rationale for therapies and what the patient and you, the caregiver, can expect to achieve by using these therapies. We should note that not all patients diagnosed with bipolar disorder will receive the same treatment because their symptoms may be different and their ability to tolerate the side effects of the medications will vary. It depends where on the bipolar spectrum the patient is diagnosed. Are they bipolar I, bipolar II, cyclothymic, or bipolar NOS? We will give some guidance as to what therapies to expect from each of these disorders.

It is essential that the patient maintains their treatment. One of the key roles of the caregiver is to encourage the patient to take their medications as prescribed by their doctor and attend psychotherapy if it is prescribed. For the hospitalized patient, the hospital staff will take care of these responsibilities, but as soon as the patient is under your care, it becomes your responsibility. Medication should never be discontinued without first consulting your primary care provider because the symptoms that return after stopping medication can be much more difficult to treat. If the side effects of the medication become intolerable, see the provider and ask them to change the medication.

Mood changes can occur even when the patient is taking their medication. When this happens, you should report the nature and the severity of the change to the doctor immediately as they may be able to intervene to adjust the medication and prevent a major episode from occurring. Also, do not forget to keep a chart of all these episodes so that you have a complete record of the patient's symptoms and the timing of when they occurred. The chart will help you to better understand what is happening and it will help the doctor to better manage the patient's symptoms.

Alcohol and drug abuse are one of the symptoms of bipolar disorder. If the patient starts to abuse these substances, it is the role of the caregiver to discourage such use and prevent access to alcohol and drugs if at all possible. If abuse occurs despite your efforts, see the doctor so that the abuse can be treated at the same time as the bipolar disorder.

Drug Therapy (Psychotherapeutic Agents, Psychopharma-cological Agents)
The goal of drug therapy is to remove the symptoms of the disorder completely. However, this rarely happens in practice because of the imperfect nature of medications and the side effects that they induce. Managing the symptoms so that the patient can lead a more-or-less normal life is about the best we can expect to achieve.

We noted earlier that disorders in the bipolar spectrum are long term, often lasting the patient's entire life. This means that the treatment they receive will also usually be of long duration, many years or forever.

Most patients will require a combination of medications to control this disease. The use of a single medication, or "monotherapy", is the exception. Monotherapy is often only the first step, depending on the severity of the patient's symptoms.

Once the course of drug therapy is started, the patient and the caregiver, whenever possible, will visit the doctor weekly or biweekly depending on the severity of the symptoms. If the symptoms are extremely severe, daily visits to the doctor may be in order. The visits are necessary so the doctor can monitor the progress of the drug therapy and observe the general well-being of the patient. It may take several weeks before the full effects of the medication are seen.

Bipolar disorder is a spectrum of disorders ranging from severe depression to mania and everything in between. Because there is a need to control this wide range of symptoms, it is usual for the patient to be prescribed more than one medication. The kinds of medication, their purpose, and the details of some of the most commonly prescribed medications are provided later in this chapter, but first we will consider the rationale for drug therapy.

While the causes of bipolar disorder are unknown, there is a basic assumption that the chemical balance in the brain is altered in those suffering from the disease, particularly in the regions of the brain responsible for controlling mood, emotion, motivation, and emotional motivation with memory. The brain region responsible is called the limbic system, an area that includes the amygdala, nucleus accumbens, hippocampus, hypothalamus, and several areas of the cortex. (A more detailed description is provided in Chapter 10 for those of you interested in the scientific and medical basis of bipolar disorder.) The assumption that an imbalance in brain chemicals is responsible for the symptoms of bipolar disorder is reasonably well founded because drugs that are known to modify the functioning of the neurons in the brain are effective in alleviating or worsening the symptoms of bipolar and other disorders.

Rational Basis of Drug Therapy

When considering the plan of treatment for the patient with bipolar disorder, it is necessary to take the entire spectrum of the disease into account because isolating and treating one part of the disease, particularly depression, and treating only one part, may have strong adverse effects for the patient. For example, many bipolar patients will be catapulted into mania when treated only with antidepressants (i.e., in the absence of a mood stabilizer).

There are several treatment protocols or algorithms, as they tend to be called, in regular use. These algorithms have been developed over many years of experience in managing patients with bipolar disorder, and they give primary care providers and psychiatrists a good guide as to which medications to prescribe and when to prescribe them.

The algorithms commonly cited in the medical literature are:

o The Texas Medical Algorithm Project — TMAP or TIMA
o The Expert Consensus Series
o American Psychiatric Association Guidelines
o Canadian Network for Mood and Anxiety Treatment (CANMAT) Guidelines for the Management of Patients with Bipolar

It is indicative of the difficulty and complexity of diagnosing and treating disorders in the bipolar spectrum that these guidelines do not entirely agree with each other. Furthermore, only the CANMAT guidelines attempt to give some direction for treatment of bipolar II as well as bipolar I disorder. The others focus only on bipolar I disorder. None of them are helpful in the treatment of cyclothymia or bipolar NOS.

The recommended medications from these studies propose the use of the medications as a series of options. They have the first option (first choice and most likely to help), followed by a second option, third option, etc. The premise is that if one drug or one combination of drugs does not work, keep going until you find the most beneficial drug or combination of drugs that help the specific patient. As you may imagine, this means that you probably will not find the right combination of medications for your patient on the first try. Have patience and do not get discouraged if the first few tries do not work. It is worth the wait to find the right solution.

Bipolar I Therapy
For the most part, doctors agree that the first option for treatment of bipolar I and bipolar II disorders is to first prescribe a mood stabilizer. There is no consensus as to what a mood stabilizer is. For the purpose of this discussion, a mood stabilizer reduces or eliminates the symptoms of acute episodes of depression, mania, and hypomania, and helps to prevent these episodes from occurring. Also, the mood stabilizer does not make either depression or mania worse and does not increase the frequency of mood cycling (these are side effects of some other therapies). Drugs considered to be traditional mood stabilizers and effective to reduce the symptoms of bipolar are:

- o Lithium (Eskalith, Lithane, Lithobid, Lithonate, Lithotabs)
- o Valproic Acid (Divalproex, Depakote, Depakene, Epival)
- o Carbamazepine (Tegretol)
- o Olanzapine (Zyprexa)

as well as the class of drugs called atypical antipsychotics:

- o Quetiapine (Seroquel)
- o Aripiprazole (Abilify)
- o Olanzapine (Zyprexa)
- o Risperidone (Risperdal)
- o Ziprasidone (Geodon)
- o Clozapine (Clozaril)

Antidepressants are widely prescribed, usually in combination with a mood stabilizer or an atypical antipsychotic, although caution is urged in the use of antidepressants in treating bipolar I and bipolar II disorders. Examples of the more commonly prescribed antidepressants are:

- o Selective serotonin reuptake inhibitors (SSRIs)
    - Fluoxetine (Prozac)
    - Sertraline (Zoloft)
    - Paroxetine (Paxil)
    - Fluvoxamine (Luvox)
    - Citalopram (Celexa)
    - Escitalopram (Lexapro)
- o Other antidepressants
    - Nefazodone (Serzone)
    - Trazodone (Desyrel)
    - Mirtazapine (Remeron)
    - Bupropion (Wellbutrin)
    - Venlaxafine (Effexor)
    - Duloxetine (Cymbalta)
- o Heterocyclic antidepressants
    - Imipramine (Tofranil, Janimine)
    - Amitryptiline (Elavil)
    - Nortryptiline (Aventyl, Pamelor)
    - Desipramine (Norpramin, Pertofrane)
    - Clomipramine (Anafranil)
    - Maprotiline (Ludiomil)
    - Amoxapine (Asendin)

- o Monoamineoxidase inhibitors (MAOIs)
  - Phenelzine (Nardil)
  - Tranylcypromine (Parnate)
  - Moclobemide (Manerix)

If the patient is having trouble sleeping or maintaining a normal sleep schedule, they can be prescribed tranquillizers or sleep aids:

- o Tranquilizers
  - Diazepam (Valium)
  - Lorazepam (Ativan)
  - Alprazolam (Xanax)
  - Clonazepam (Klonoprin)
- o Sleep aids
  - Xoldipem (Ambien)
  - Temazepam (Restoril)
  - Zaleplon (Sonata)
  - Eszopiclone (Lunesta)
  - Ramelteon (Rozerem)

Both CANMAT and the Expert Consensus Guidelines propose a mood stabilizer–antidepressant combination as a first option, despite the risk of switching into mania. This is not the case with TIMA, which recommends this combination only after three prior treatments have failed. The problem associated with antidepressants is that they may induce rapid cycling in patients with a history of rapid cycling and, therefore, antidepressants should not be used in these patients or in patients with a history of severe mania. On the other hand, for patients whose main symptoms are depression with mild mania or hypomania, antidepressants may be considered as a first option.

Note: TIMA is considered to be the best guideline to date.

TIMA guidelines divide treatment algorithms for mania and depression depending on the primary presenting symptoms. For depression, Lamotrigine (Lamictal) is recommended with the addition of an antimanic medication if there is a recent history of mania or hypomania. Often, either lithium or an atypical antipsychotic *with* (not without) depressive properties will be used.

For mania, lithium, valproic acid, or one of the atypical antipsychotics (except Olanzapine or Clozapine) are considered first choice, then combinations if a better response is needed.

Bipolar II Therapy

For the treatment of bipolar II disorder, the CANMAT first choices include lithium or Lamictal. Second options include an antimanic agent with an antidepressant or a double combination from a choice of lithium, Lamictal, Depakote, or an atypical antipsychotic. They did not rule out antidepressant monotherapy, although only as a third option (along with Tegretol, an atypical antipsychotic, or electroconvulsive therapy – see below).

Cyclothymia and Bipolar NOS Therapy

Unfortunately, there is limited research into the treatment of cyclothymia and bipolar NOS. The guideline for the doctor or psychiatrist seems to be to look at the symptoms and treat accordingly. While this does not seem to be very satisfactory from the patient's point of view, it is the best we can do at the present time. In many cases, prescribing a mood stabilizer such as lithium is a logical first option that has been shown to be effective.

Side Effects

All drugs have side effects and you should ask the doctor about the side effects of the medications prescribed to your patient. You should monitor the patient's reaction to all medications, write them in the patient's chart, and report them to the doctor. People respond to medication in different ways and it is difficult for the doctor to know just how any one patient may react to a medication. If the side effects become unbearable, ask the doctor to change the medication or adjust the dosage. If there are special circumstances, such as pregnancy, comorbid illnesses, or prior (family) history of bad experience with particular medications, let the doctor know before he starts the patient on a medication.

Bipolar Therapy with Therapies for Comorbid Illnesses

As we have noted, all drugs have some side effects. Additional side effects may be noticed when a patient is taking multiple drugs for bipolar disorder and comorbid illnesses. These side effects are the result of drug-drug interactions, meaning that one drug is interacting with another drug to produce an effect other than the one intended for each of the drugs if given separately. Doctors and pharmacists are generally aware of possible drug-drug interactions and will avoid them when the effects are negative to the patient. If you see any reaction in the patient from multiple drug therapy, be sure to notify the doctor so that the medications can be adjusted or changed when necessary.

Electroconvulsive Therapy

Electroconvulsive therapy (ECT) is also considered a mood-stabilizing treatment and has been used successfully to manage severe depression and mania. ECT is generally considered as a treatment of last resort when the patient's condition is extremely bad or suicidal. Patients are hospitalized and receive several treatments spread over a few weeks. Relapses are common and the patient will require follow-up treatments. The response to up to ten electroconvulsive treatments is usually dramatic and may be lifesaving. Side effects of ECT can be quite serious including short-term memory loss and, in a few cases, long-term memory loss.

Since ECT is a somewhat controversial therapy, you should discuss it with the doctor and with the patient. If the patient does not want ECT no matter what their condition, you should make sure their wishes are known and included in the advance directive document we advised you to draw up in Chapter 4.

Psychotherapy (Talking Therapy or Counseling)
In conjunction with medications, psychotherapy enables the bipolar I and some bipolar II patients to understand and manage the symptoms of their disease and to cope with everyday life. It may reduce hospitalizations, improve functioning, and lead to better maintenance of the patient's mood and behavior. Through education, the patient and caregiver can learn to identify the signs and symptoms leading to relapses and thereby "head off" some of these relapses. Psychotherapy should be adopted for all patients diagnosed with bipolar I disorder and for selected patients diagnosed with bipolar II disorder, and may be conducted by a psychiatrist or a licensed therapist, social worker, or counselor working with a psychiatrist. Psychotherapy is not usually recommended for patients with cyclothymia or bipolar NOS, although family or couples therapy can be of use to resolve interpersonal problems in the cyclothymic patient.

Patients should each receive an individualized plan related to their specific needs and the plan should detail the number, type, and frequency of sessions with the therapist. The most benefit will be gained by the patient attending all the sessions and it is the responsibility of the caregiver to make sure that the patient complies with the plan. The psychiatrist or therapist will determine how long the sessions should continue, but long-term therapy is usually not necessary.

There have been several psychotherapeutic approaches studied specifically for the bipolar patient. These studies were designed to detect and note discrete episodes in advance of full-blown symptoms. As such, they are mostly relevant to the bipolar I patient, although some bipolar II patients may also benefit.

Almost all patients, even those taking medications, will suffer relapses. One of the main goals in psychotherapy for the bipolar patient is to identify the signs that lead up to an episode so that the patient can learn to manage their disorder. The approaches include education about bipolar disorder involving the patient, caregiver, and doctor, and the studies show quite impressively that education will reduce the number of relapses resulting in a major episode in the bipolar I patient.

Other foci in psychotherapy include:

o The need to continue on medications even during periods of wellness
o Improving relationships
o Stress management and problem solving
o Developing daily schedules for sleep, exercise, and other activities

The different approaches that the psychotherapist might take that have been shown to be effective in bipolar I and could also be helpful in bipolar II disorder include:

1. Detecting signs and symptoms (prodrome detection) — Involves the therapist discussing with the patient their recollections of the signs and symptoms that occurred before previous manic and depressive episodes. If these signs and symptoms can be noted and learned, they can be readily recognized when they occur again. An index card describing the signs and symptoms as a memory refresher is a good idea for the patient to carry around and for the caregiver to keep available.
2. Psychoeducation — Involves teaching the patient and caregiver about bipolar disorder, its treatment, and the

support that is available. Being educated about the disease and knowing what to expect has been shown to reduce the number of relapses in patients because they are able to intervene before the relapse becomes full blown.

3. Cognitive therapy (cognitive behavioral therapy) — Involves the therapist working with the patient to help them change negative and inappropriate thought patterns associated with mania and depression.

4. Interpersonal and social rhythm therapy (IPRST) — Focuses on teaching the patient how to improve interpersonal relationships and how to build regular schedules of activity and sleep into their daily routine.

5. Family-focused therapy (FFT) and integrated FFT/IPSRT — In addition to IPRST, the therapist focuses on reducing the level of stress associated with the patient in the family circle. Stress may both contribute to and be a consequence of bipolar disorder.

Stress Avoidance

Stress is a problem for anyone with a mood disorder and anything that can be done to avoid having the patient get into a stressful situation should be attempted whether the stress is work related, at home, or family oriented. Psychotherapy can be very beneficial in identifying stress factors and learning how to avoid them or how to cope with them.

Homeopathy/Nutropathy

Although these therapies have not been proven to be effective clinically, common homeopathic remedies for depression include *Arsenicum album*, *Aurum metallicum*, *Calcarea carbonica*, *Causticum*, *Cimicifuga*, *Ignatia amara*, *Kali phosphoricum*, *Natrum carbonicum*, *Natrum muriaticum*, *Pulsatilla*, *Sepia*, St. John's Wort, Valerian, and *Staphysagria*.

Treatment for Children and Adolescents

One of the difficulties when diagnosing bipolar disorder in children is that the diagnosis requires at least one episode of mania, hypomania, or mixed state. However, the most common presentation, especially in adolescents, is depression without a clear history of mania or hypomania. Another confusing feature is the coexistence of ADD/ADHD. This has been reported to be as high as 80% in children with bipolar disorder.

Very few studies have been conducted on the treatment of bipolar disorder in children. Therefore, treatment for children tends to mimic treatment for adults. As with the adult population, the goal of treatment in children is to first stabilize mood and then manage the symptoms of bipolar disorder. Treatment includes both medication and psychotherapy or counseling. It is very important that you find a doctor or psychiatrist experienced in childhood bipolar disorder because the symptoms are hard to diagnose and they are different than in adults, particularly in the manic episodes (see Chapter 3). Equally important for the children is the management of their environment so that their home and school lives are as low stress as possible, and so that the child's support group, usually family and friends, is constantly available to them. Of course, this implies that the family and friends are well educated in what to expect from the bipolar child. Ideally, the whole family should be involved in the child's treatment plan, but it is essential that the caregiver be involved actively. The caregiver can identify external resources or support groups to help the child, and can answer their questions and help them to identify the signs and symptoms leading up to a major manic or depressive episode. The caregiver makes sure that the child takes their medications at the appropriate times and makes sure that they show up for appointments with their doctor and therapist.

If the child is diagnosed early and receives the appropriate medications, psychotherapy or counseling, and the support of family and friends, they have a good chance of managing their symptoms so that they occur with less severity, duration, and frequency.

Medications for children focus first on stabilizing mood and lithium is often the drug of choice. It is important to start the child on medication as soon as possible to prevent serious consequences such as suicide, self-harm, and failure at school. Generally speaking, psychotherapy is not attempted until mood stabilization occurs. The process of finding the right medications for the child will be a matter of trying a medication and seeing if it works. If it does, continue with the medication; if it does not, then try something else. This process will repeat until the right medications are found. The process may take months or even longer to complete, and the child may end up taking several different medications daily to control their symptoms. Remember that it is all worthwhile because the consequences of not treating the child may include suicide, substance abuse, and failure at school and in relationships. The kinds of medications that will be used are the same as for adults, namely mood stabilizers, antipsychotics, antianxiety agents, sleeping pills, etc. However, a strong degree of caution is urged in the use of antidepressants in children. Antidepressants may induce manic symptoms in the bipolar child if a mood stabilizer is not already being taken. Because many bipolar children are misdiagnosed as ADHD for which antidepressants may be prescribed, the caregiver should be vigilant and prepared to question the doctor if antidepressants without a mood stabilizer are prescribed, especially if there is a family history of bipolar disorder.

Psychotherapy for Children
The doctor should be able to refer you to a psychiatrist, licensed psychologist, or clinical social worker with

experience in child psychotherapy. It is absolutely essential that the therapist is experienced in working with childhood bipolar disorder. The doctor and the psychotherapist should work together to find the right balance of medications and therapy for the child. There should be an emphasis on cognitive therapy and interpersonal therapy to help the child manage their negative thoughts and relationships. A multifamily support group may be recommended to encourage interaction between families with bipolar children and to support each other.

A Cautionary Note

The bipolar child has an illness that can result in self-harm, destructive rages, and even suicide when symptoms are severe. It should be common sense that this child should never be left unsupervised, but in this day and age with so much pressure on working parents, it happens. As the caregiver, you must make preparations to make sure that the child is kept out of harms way and is supervised constantly. Should the family situation result in disagreements between parents as to how the child should be treated, remember that it is the child who must come first and their well-being must be uppermost in your mind. If parental differences cannot be resolved, it is possible to get a court order to ensure the proper treatment for the child.

Other Treatments

Nutritional Supplements and Diet

A few studies have shown that some nutritional supplements may be beneficial to the bipolar patient. These supplements should never take the place of medications, but they can probably do no harm and may help if taken with the medications. Supplements that may be beneficial are α-omega fatty acids from fish such as salmon; vitamins B1, B2, B6, B9, C; as well as magnesium, tryptophan, and SAM-e. Other vitamins and minerals have been suggested as well. Ask the doctor for advice before adding any of these supplements to the diet.

A good diet is essential to normal body functioning including the functioning of the brain. You can consult a nutritionist to find out what would be considered a healthy diet for your patient. Be aware and make note of any reactions that your patient may have to food additives.

Acupuncture
There is some evidence that acupuncture may benefit the bipolar patient, but you should consult the doctor before embarking on this route of treatment.

Exercise
Many studies have found that daily or regular exercise is beneficial, even working as well as antidepressants. Exercise is part of a healthy lifestyle that we are striving to maintain for the patient. Encourage them to exercise regularly. As little as 20 minutes three times a week will aid muscle tone, increase energy levels, and will help the patient to develop regular sleep patterns.

Sleep
It is important for the patient to develop a sleep pattern that coincides with the family schedule. Eight hours of sleep during the night and waking up at a normal time will benefit the patient and the family. A lack of sleep in the bipolar patient may trigger a manic episode and will affect their daily performance. Too much sleep can also affect their mood, so get the patient onto a regular sleep schedule and if it proves difficult, ask the doctor for medication to help the patient sleep.

6. The Effective Caregiver

So far, we have described and discussed the bipolar spectrum disorders. The patient with cyclothymia or bipolar NOS will require much less care than the patient with bipolar I or bipolar II disorders. For this reason, the majority of the comments in this chapter focus on the caregiver for the patient with bipolar I disorder.

As a caregiver for someone with a medical disability or illness, the task can be challenging, emotionally taxing, and overwhelming. As a caregiver for someone with a psychiatric illness, there will be different challenges as these diseases alter the mental state of the patient so that their moods and behavior become abnormal and more difficult to manage. Also, these diseases are often incurable and require lifelong treatment. Bipolar spectrum disorders are such diseases and although they are treatable, they require the individual to submit themselves to a lifelong routine of taking medication to control the depressive and manic episodes. Counseling may also be required for bipolar I and some bipolar II patients.

Among the challenges you can anticipate from the person affected by bipolar disorder is their refusal to continue to see their clinician, or to stop taking or refuse to take their medications. Without medication, the patient will suffer relapses and you, the caregiver, must make it a high priority to learn how to overcome these challenges so that the patient takes their medications and sees their doctor on the prescribed schedule. In this chapter, we will give you some suggestions about how to overcome these challenges.

Another challenge you may face that needs to be overcome by you, your family, and the patient is the stigma associated with mental illness. The stigma in our society derives largely from ignorance and the best way to overcome ignorance is to educate. First, you must educate yourself. However, even before you do that, you should accept that you are caring for a person with a mental illness. Do not hide from it and do not feel any guilt because of it, because you are among millions who are learning to deal with this illness.

For you, the caregiver, these challenges will pale in comparison to the heavy stress and emotional toll this disease may cause you in the course of your relationship with the one you love. Your task as caregiver can push you to the breaking point where you may feel isolated and depressed yourself, or you feel hopeless, as if you are the only one and your family is the only family affected by this devastating disease. Take comfort in the fact that you are not alone and there are many families that share this situation and the experience of caregiving for someone with bipolar disorder.

As you progress along your journey as a caregiver, you will learn how to cope effectively as you become more aware of your personal limitations and by educating yourself about the disease. This is a process and, in time, you will learn to deal with the intensity of stresses, strains, and the ups and downs of bipolar disorder. Once you learn how to recognize the signs and symptoms of impending depression, mania, or hypomania, you will be able to prepare for the upcoming episodes and your life will be more in your control. The transformation that you will have to experience is one that will help you to navigate the course of bipolar disorder, by giving yourself completely to the process of learning and allowing yourself to understand that this is a disease that the affected person cannot manage by themselves.

As with any job or task, you must be educated or trained for the job you are about to perform. Caregiving requires you to be prepared and for you to be educated as best you can about bipolar disorder. By reading *Bipolar Essentials*, you have taken that first step, but it does not end here. There is so much more to learn outside of these pages and some of this information will be learned through performing your role as a caregiver. Some will come from observing the one you are caring for and some may come from interaction with medical professionals or support groups. You must be committed to learning. By educating yourself, you can reduce the stress you will experience as you will have better coping skills and will be able to be proactive in times of mania or depression. As well, understanding the disease will help you to reduce the amount of resentment you may feel. Keep in mind that the person you love with the disease is not responsible for the disease they were born with. They did not ask for this disease, nor do they want it. By learning about bipolar disorder, you can help that person to cope and feel loved by someone who accepts them for who they really are, rather than just a person with a disease.

A great place to start is with something you do not need to learn how to have — hope. Be positive, be optimistic, and look forward to the "normal" times. Remember that bipolar disorder is, for the most part, a treatable disease and the patient can be stabilized. Having hope and understanding that the phases of the disease are only temporary and shall pass will help you to cope while caring for the bipolar patient.

Once you accept hope and accept your role as caregiver, make a time to speak with the primary care provider and the pharmacist. Ask the provider specific questions about the medication your loved one is taking, learn how the medications work, what they do, and why the doctor believes they are the best. You should also glean as much information as possible on what to look for when the patient is becoming depressed, hypomanic, or manic. Seek the pharmacist's advice about drug interactions, potential side effects, and any other indications that you should look for should there be any adverse reaction to the medication. Your patient will probably take more than one medication so it is important for you to be knowledgeable and vigilant. Remember that your physician is there to make the diagnosis, prescribe medications/ treatment, and to follow the patient through their disease. The pharmacist is the expert on what the medications help or harm. Realize that you will be going through a process of trial and error while finding the best course of treatment, and this process will be frustrating, particularly during the times that multiple medications are being tried.

Having a network of support is very important to your education about bipolar disorder. Finding local support groups and interacting with others who live with a bipolar spectrum disorder can help in this process as you will encounter seasoned veterans of the bipolar battlefield. You will learn the best offense to prepare for the worst, from individuals who have been there and done that. You realize that your friends will not understand bipolar disorder, so it is important to believe that the support group is there to do exactly what it is intended to do, support you. You must accept that this group wants to help care for you and get you through the difficult times.

This is a Family Disease
As you have learned in previous chapters, bipolar spectrum disorders are hereditary diseases, diseases prevalent within families. While this is true in the medical sense, it is also true that one family member's mood disorder affects each and every person in the family and possibly your extended families. It is heartbreaking to see the one you love deteriorate into a state where their mood is sullen or melancholy, and it is exciting to see them happy or elated. These ups and downs will put strains on your relationship because this disease is a

rollercoaster and, often times, you are the carnival ride operator that has to help manage the ride or the cycles of bipolar disorder.

It is your responsibility as the primary caregiver to call the immediate family together and educate them about what bipolar disorder is, what it is not, what you as a caregiver will need from the family, what the family's role is in its entirety, as well as the responsibility of each individual member. The family will need to understand the early warning signs of manic or depressive episodes, what the disease does to the person affected, and what the difference is between manic, hypomanic, and depressive episodes. As well, you will need to explain the course of treatment and side effects of the medications. Most importantly, you must discuss how each person can participate in the caregiving role and how they can support you. Remember that it is not irresponsible or weak to accept help or ask for help. In order to help this process of educating and discussing these topics with your family, you should consult a therapist who specializes in mood disorders to help oversee the family meeting. They can help your family understand this complex and daunting task of caregiving. If everyone understands bipolar disorder and its effect on your family member, you can come to terms with the disease, avoid the stigma attached to mental illness, and help to educate others who may be ignorant or fearful of the disease.

Being a Partner in Treatment

Your role as caregiver will be more satisfying if you can build an understanding relationship with your patient so that you become a partner in treatment. Of course, this does not mean that you have to take medications too, but rather you become a supportive partner, a coach when needed, and a crutch on which they can lean in the times of despair. It means that you can help by finding qualified clinicians (psychiatrist/ psychologist), scheduling appointments, keeping track of any errors or missed doses of medication, reordering medications, making sure they take their medications, and keeping a behavior record when you see changes. If you do find changes, you can report that to the clinician. You are the historian. By being the partner, you can develop the early warning system, the battlefield logic to always be prepared with a new strategy.

Coping Methods: Things to Recognize and Consider

There will be times when you feel the loss of your loved one when they are suffering an episode of mania or depression. Many times, due to the tremendous emotional burdens you experience, caregivers will attempt to find an excuse or "cure" for the illness. If this occurs, try to remember that it is not your responsibility to cure the person, it is your responsibility to be there to help them during their times of need, when they are unable to function, cope, or care for themselves properly. There is no one to blame for the disease and you cannot cure a neurological or mood disorder, so focus on what you can do to help.

Relapses may occur even if the person is compliant with their medications. This may be unexpected and hard for you to understand, but you should inform the primary care provider of these changes. Despite the medications and your diligence in helping your patient, the symptoms of the disease may get worse. To deal with this, you must separate the person from the disorder. Look into the person, find the love in your heart that you have for them, and find the positive within the negative. Love the person, hate the disorder, and remember that medications can cause side effects (such as listlessness) so you should separate that from the person as well. This is difficult to do, but if you can accomplish the task of loving the person for who they are, not what they have become because of their illness, you will be able to cope much better and reduce your stress levels.

Asking for help from friends or family or your support group is essential to your well-being and your ability to cope with your role as caregiver. There will be times when you feel overwhelmed and your stress level is unhealthy, and this is when you need help. Taking care of yourself is important, not only for you, but also for your patient. If you cannot cope, your patient will suffer even more, so make sure that you have the support of your family, friends, and the organizations available to you to get some respite for yourself and recharge your batteries.

You may have to re-evaluate your expectations of the person that you are caring for and realize that they have limited capabilities. You should set clear guidelines, boundaries, and crystal-clear limits of what your expectations are for the patient and yourself so there is a mutual understanding as to what behaviors are acceptable.

During time to yourself, you may experience strong emotions such as guilt, fear, denial, grief, anger, confusion, sadness, or hurt. These are natural feelings, and you must embrace them and commit to accepting the situation you are in. It is said that healing occurs when one accepts and has understanding. At times, it will be hard to accept the unusual behavior that you will experience, but remember that irritability and unusual behavior are symptoms of bipolar disorder. During these times or times of depression or mania, you may be subjected to verbal abuse from your patient, but do not take these words to heart. It is not personal, it is a disease talking. Allow yourself and the one you love some dignity, and treat yourself to a laugh every day. Keep a sense of humor and believe in yourself most of all.

Suicide or Threat of Suicide
Suicide is a reality that one faces with bipolar patients. The potential is there for self-harm and attempted suicide, and without intervention they may be successful. You must be

vigilant and listen for signs that they may be considering hurting themselves. Make sure that family and friends know that they must report any such signs to you no matter how trivial they think they might be. In particular, you must explain to siblings the seriousness with which they must take these signs and report them to you.

Sometimes though, a threat of suicide can be a cry for help. Do not be afraid to ask the patient if they are contemplating suicide or hurting themselves. Keeping open communication will help you both to cope. Often times, the person with bipolar disorder is looking for an escape from the consequences of the disorder and, through this time of hopelessness, their judgment and thinking will be impaired. They certainly may not recognize that they are viewing their world through bipolar glasses.

The Disorder vs. the Person You Know?
The person you know with bipolar disorder becomes the representation of the disease by the expression of negative symptoms such as mood, actions, or words that are a result of the disorder. In time, you may find yourself angry with this person or you may lash out and believe that they are responsible for your unhappiness, stress, or inability to function. Check your reality! You are responsible for your feelings, your reactions, and your interpretations. You are not the victim in this case. If any one is victimized, it is the person with bipolar disorder; they are the victim of the symptoms of the disease.

You may find it difficult to separate yourself during times of mania when the person is irrational and fragmented, or during a major depressive episode. It is easy to blame the person for these situations. Reality check! This is not the person, but the disease at work. To disassociate yourself, you must first educate yourself on the symptoms, behaviors, and mood changes associated with bipolar disorder and ask yourself if this behavior is consistent with the true character of the person you are caring for.

You are the caregiver. You represent the stability and safety for this person, but more importantly, you are their coach. To get through bipolar disorder, you and the one you are caring for must form a mental alliance. In order for you to form an alliance, you must first be able to recognize the difference in the person vs. the disease. Do not be tempted to blame every unacceptable behavior on the disease. They probably had some bad habits before the symptoms of bipolar were evident and those bad habits persist, but they have nothing to do with bipolar disorder. If you do blame everything on the disease, you will devalue the importance of the person's ability to think on their own or diminish the identity of self. It is equally important to make sure that you are not attributing too little to the symptoms of bipolar disorder as this can be just as damaging to your patient.

For you to disassociate the disease from the person, you will need to reflect on the person you remember. When you are starting to blame the person for their behavior or mood, it is beneficial to look to the past for relief, to remember what the person was like before they were symptomatic. Ask yourself if the person is similar to who they were then or have they changed. If so, in what ways? What were their behaviors like then and how are they different now?

You may want to keep or make a photo album or scrapbook of the wonderful times you shared before the symptoms began. When you find yourself blaming the person, take a step back, go to a quiet place, and calm yourself by looking through the scrapbook. See the person for who they are, not for the disease they have.

Positive Thinking and Realistic Expectations

The way you think has much to do with what you do as you approach your role as a caregiver. You will be confronting your own preconceived notions of what to expect, you will often be wrong, you will say the wrong things, you will do the wrong things, but consider this as part of your learning process to be a caregiver to the bipolar patient. There is no rule book, no certain path you can follow. It is a learning process, a trial by fire.

Do not give up, you can do it. Have faith in yourself, stay positive, have realistic expectations of what can be achieved, and believe that you can live as normal a life as possible with someone who has been diagnosed with bipolar disorder. Remember, with compliance to medication, therapy, and positive lifestyle, you can, for the most part, manage the symptoms of bipolar disorder, resulting in a rewarding life together. However, you must adhere to the treatment plan to make that life possible.

The realistic expectations you should have include the following:

o Neither you nor the patient is responsible for their illness, but together you have a good chance to control the symptoms.
o You have joint responsibility for being vigilant, getting education and therapy, and sticking to routine and medication compliance.
o Medication compliance is required to help prevent relapses of mania and depression.
o The patient cannot overcome this disease by themselves. They need your help and the help of their clinicians. They need support from friends and family.
o They are always vulnerable to mood episodes and symptoms may occur even when the prescribed medications are being taken.

o At times, the one you are caring for may not want your help. At times, they may refuse and get angry. You must be understanding, validating, and loving.

o You must remember when to back off. Getting angry or attacking the person you are caring for is disastrous. Recognize your own reactions and feelings.

o Be flexible and realize that you will need to adjust your expectations and lifestyle to help the person you love fight bipolar symptoms.

o Stay diligent in your record keeping and analysis of the person's moods and symptoms. When times are good, you may want to let your guard down, but you can never do so when you are caring for someone with bipolar disorder because warning signs of a relapse can happen at any time.

With realistic expectations, you can maintain your stress levels and find peace within the storm of emotions called bipolar disorder.

Recognize Impending Episodes

"Proactive" is a word that should be a part of your vocabulary after reading *Bipolar Essentials*. The more you are able to understand the signs of impending depression or mania, the more likely you will be able to help your patient avoid social or occupational dysfunction and make life easier for yourself.

By recognizing mood and behavioral changes and by helping the person recognize these changes themselves and alerting their clinician (especially the talk therapist for bipolar I patients), you can help to reduce the impact of the symptoms and maintain a healthy productive life for the patient and yourself.

The way to learn the signs of impending episodes is to observe your patient and keep good records of their mood and behavioral changes. Discuss these with the medical team to establish what is important. Once these signs have been identified, you will be better prepared to educate the patient and be proactive with therapy. You should be the coach on your patient's team, leading the way to a better life.

Communicating with the Bipolar Patient

When communicating with someone who is affected by a bipolar spectrum disorder, there are specific steps that you have to take to make the communication process easier. First and foremost, you must be honest, but not cruel. Keep in mind the basic premise, "Do unto others as you would want done to you." Would you want someone patronizing you or saying something bluntly that comes across as cruel? Think before you speak. When you are talking to someone who is manic or in a depressive state, remember that they may not be able to speak clearly or hear the things you say clearly. In order to lessen the risk of misinterpretation, use clear, short, and direct sentences. If you elaborate too much, run on and on, repeat yourself, or talk in circles, they may tune you out. Also, try to cover one topic at a time and when that topic is finished, move on to the next until the conversation is finished. Give clear directions and remember to be as specific as you can when doing so.

Environmental factors can hinder the communication process and it is imperative to keep the stimulation level to a minimum. Imagine for a moment that you are in a room filled with a hundred TVs, all on. There is a gang of people talking loudly and there is other ambient noise. You cannot leave, you cannot get away from the noise. Ask yourself, "How would I feel?" Chances are that you would feel a bit anxious. It is much worse for the person with bipolar disorder.

If you are to discuss a matter, never talk in a loud voice or in an insistent manner as this will immediately turn the person off. If you find yourself getting angry, as frustrated as you are and as much as you want to blow your top, you need to walk away and keep your comments to yourself. If you make accusations, criticize, or call names, this can be painfully deflating for anyone, let alone someone who has suffered a mental shift or breakdown. Wait until you have calmed down before returning. Go talk to a friend, go for a walk, take a shower, or take a drive... your choice.

There may be times that you want to discuss something or just have a general conversation with your loved one, but you find that they appear to be uncommunicative or withdrawn. Back off and give them the space they need. Return later, you will have a better chance of communicating when they are ready to speak.

In any conversation or communication, we all interpret what we want to hear and we fail to assimilate or just forget some of the things that have been said. Imagine for a moment a time when you were very stressed, people came at you with all kinds of questions, the kids wanted your attention, the dog wanted to play, the cat needed to be petted, and your significant other or parent asked you to perform a task. Did you remember to do everything asked of you? Chances are that you did not and you had to be asked more than once for the things that slipped by. This is what happens frequently to the person living with bipolar disorder. You need to be patient and you will need to repeat your instructions, directions, or things that you said over again. Remember that this is a neurological illness that affects the way the brain operates and it means that the person's ability to process information may not be what you expect from a person without the disease. If you need to repeat yourself, be pleasant. Most of all, remember that a hug, a touch, and positive reinforcement are very helpful. Below, you will find a list of things you can say or do that will encourage positive reinforcement for the one you care for with bipolar disorder. As well, you will find a list of things you never want to say to someone in a state of depression or mania.

Do You Really Want to Take It Personally?
Who told you that life was all about you, that the world revolved around you? No one did! You are not that special, none of us are. We are individuals that share a world, share our lives with the ones we love, and ultimately, we are creatures that cohabit and have emotions. Those closest to us are the ones that can hurt us the most, and many times a hurt or an emotion is a response to something we do not want to hear or something that is said that we do not agree with and we grow angry. We are human beings and you may find that your happiness or sadness is tied to the ones that you love the most.

As a caregiver, you may feel the pain of the one you are caring for. There are times you will feel like a failure, but do not fret; you are strong and can thrive. There will also be times when the one you are caring for will lash out at you. Your reaction may be frustration, denial, anger, or a sense of failure that could lead to resentment and bitterness towards the person with bipolar disorder. This is where the concept of separating the person from the disease really comes into play because, many times, when the person is feeling dejected, irritable, impatient, or suffering with paranoia, they are showing symptoms of the illness. Finding valid responses each time for these situations can be difficult, but separate the person from the disease and separate you from their world. You are not the cause of their issues, regardless of what the person says to you (unless you are verbally abusive by yelling or saying hurtful words). Be kind, but firm, even in the most difficult situations. The way you react will mitigate the way the person with bipolar disorder will react to you. They also may emulate your behavior. If you are sullen, they may be sullen; if you are happy, they may be happy.

If you take these situations personally, you will significantly contribute to the reinforcement of negative behavior from the individual you are caring for. If you want to blame them, let it go. If you blame yourself, you are acting arrogantly. Do not blame, it is a wasted emotion. Take responsibility for your actions for you are in a much better position to control your reaction than the person with bipolar disorder. They cannot be held responsible for the symptoms of their disease.

Helping: You Can Do It or You Cannot Do It

Watching bipolar disorder develop in your loved one is like watching a train wreck happen. You may feel mortified that you are watching them suffer and you feel helpless and want to help, but how? You know that the one with bipolar disorder is grappling with mood swings, the physician is the one caring for general health and diagnosis, and the psychotherapist is there to listen when the person with bipolar disorder needs to talk. So where does that leave you? How can you help?

How You Can Do This

Any person, regardless of illness, can accept or deny help. They may reject your efforts for involvement. If this occurs, step back and then approach the person again. If you are overbearing, the individual with bipolar disorder may become resentful and may resist future attempts for intervention. But with a kind and gentle approach, you can offer your patient validation, understanding, supportiveness, clear directions or questions, positive reinforcement, empathy, and willingness to listen. More than likely, these are the most valuable help you can offer.

Remember to always try to have empathy and a smile, and be free of condescending tones. Approach with kindness and love with a purity of heart to truly help the person to help themselves.

Do not nag them if they are in need of help from their doctor or therapist. Nagging will only cause them to resent the help that you are offering, to rebel, or to ignore your statements. It is best to encourage and be patient. You should also keep your emotional stability in line by setting boundaries. Setting boundaries will reduce your stress and let the bipolar person know where your limits are.

What else can you do to help? Be the figurative hand holder, the support that the bipolar person needs:

- o Seek professional help from a therapist, psychiatrist, or other health care provider.
- o Be the "mood and medication accountant". Take responsibility to track moods and behavior and monitor compliance with medication and the effects of medication.
- o Be vigilant with watching for signs and symptoms of impending mood episodes. If an episode is to occur, prepare to help the person through this time.
  - Most of all, when it subsides, you need to be there for them to provide unconditional love and encouragement.
  - You can also call the person's employer to report that an illness will prevent them from coming to work. However, do not give details without the permission of the bipolar individual.
- o During times of doubt, be the "emotional coach" by supporting them with positive statements and reassurance.
- o Arrange, track, and attend doctors/therapy appointments with the person you are caring for. This does not mean that you should go into the visit with them unless it is requested by or approved by the patient and the clinician. Always ask if you can go into the visit with them, never assume.
- o If you are not able to be with the person full time, make sure to set a "contact schedule" where you will call them at certain intervals during the day. As a suggestion, call every 2–3 hours.

   o Become educated about the disease and educate friends and family.

You Cannot Do This

You are not the one with bipolar disorder. Even though you have to live with the effects of the disease and you have educated yourself about bipolar disorder, never assume that you know what the patient is going through and never tell them that you think you understand or know what they are feeling or what they need to do to get through the day. Ownership of those feelings belongs to the person with the illness. Those feelings are not for you to own. If you believe you can control the person, forget it, because it is impossible. You cannot control anything except your own reactions. You cannot take control or own an illness, situation, or issue that you do not have the power to fix. You can only empathize with them. Empathy is a gift that you give through your understanding, love, and commitment to sticking by their side through the rough times and the good times.

You cannot force this person to do anything that they do not want to do. They are an adult and if they choose not to take medication or go to see their doctor or therapist, you cannot make them. What you *can* do is encourage them to do these things so they will help to stabilize their lives and those of their family. Stepping in at the right moment to encourage them is appropriate because we know that a person with bipolar disorder is unable, at times, to make correct and prudent decisions.

What is not appropriate is for you to try to control the person and manage their lives. It is up to that person to manage their life. Ultimately, it is the bipolar person's responsibility to take ownership of their treatment plan, which includes mood tracking, medication compliance, or regular visits to therapy. But as you read previously in this chapter, you can be the "emotional coach" and the "mood and medication accountant". You can coach and assist in monitoring the person's compliance with medications, coaching them to continue therapy, keep doctors appointments, get enough rest/sleep, and avoid risky behaviors such as consumption of alcohol, caffeine, social drugs, or other mood-altering substances. Most importantly, you can coach them to be open and honest with you. Reinforce that you are there to help them and they should not be hesitant to ask for help. You are not there to be the overbearing dictator and tell them what they are to do, how to live their life, or to make decisions for them regarding their treatment.

<u>You Said What? You Did What?</u>
Psychological and emotional distress can cause a great deal of pain. As the caregiver, at times you may feel confused, guilty, angry, frustrated, depressed, hopeless, sad, or alone. For the person with bipolar disorder, those feelings are amplified significantly by a chronic illness that affects their personal and professional life every day. You both are continually adjusting to the challenges of the unpredictable nature of bipolar disorder. At times, you both may be overly sensitive, emotional, and strike out. Often times, this feeling is propagated by a sense of vulnerability because you are at the mercy of this beast of a disease. Bipolar disorder is like a wild animal, unpredictable, and this may cause great stress for you as the caregiver. The patient may be having a terrific run without any mood changes and then, "boom!" The mood change hits and it could be either depression or mania. This relapse can cause you or the person with the illness to be hypersensitive to any mention of the disease.

As the caregiver, you must be cognizant of your words and actions. If you start to make assumptions about why a relapse occurred, it will only cause more pain and distress. Follow the suggestions below to maintain equilibrium with your patient:

o Do not blame the illness for every argument, missed medication, relapse, or behavior. The illness may relapse even if the person is taking their medications continuously. If they are noncompliant with the medication, however, this may contribute to the relapse.

o Do not make blame statements. Blaming serves no purpose and are counterproductive; blame statements begin with the word "you". Instead, if something hurts you say, "I am feeling like..." or use "I've observed...." These statements can help to diffuse any blame-natured comments.

o Do not tell the person they are incapable or have a disease, they know this. If you reinforce this notion, you can cause the person to feel helpless, even dependent on you. Be encouraging.

o Do not be too insistent. Remember that this is the person's life, not yours. They make their own choices. You may want to help, but nagging them will not accomplish anything. You can remind the person of important matters, but do not go overboard. If you see something that the person is not doing, use a phrase like, "I've observed that there is..."

o Do not make threats, such as, "I'm leaving you" or "I'm going to call your doctor." If you make statements such as these, you will undermine the person's trust in you.

o Do not tell the person how they feel, how they should feel, or how they should be behaving. That is not your place and you do not really know how they feel. You can only empathize.

o Do not belittle the person by joking about their feelings, stresses, or thoughts. This can be incredibly damaging to someone's self-esteem.

o Do not make condescending statements such as, "You should have known better," "You know you can't do that," or "You'll never get any better unless you take your medications."

o Do not shame the person; there is no shame in an illness, particularly a mental illness that can cause someone to behave irrationally.

o Do not bring up the disease as the scapegoat for all the person's troubles in interpersonal or professional relationships. The disease may not be the cause, it may be that person's own behavior. We all bring life's experiences to all of our relationships and that baggage can mitigate a person's reaction or approach to a situation.

o Do not be bossy and tell the person what to do. You are not their parent (unless this is a child affected by the disease).

o Do not ever go behind the person's back and speak with their clinician or psychotherapist. This is only acceptable in case of an emergency. A therapist can only use information directly from the person in therapy. If you go behind their back and the statement is mentioned in therapy, it could undermine the trust the patient and clinician share.

Structure, Structure, Structure!
In order for someone with bipolar disorder to succeed in living a healthy and stable life, they must follow routines. These routines include getting ample sleep, eating well, exercising, complying with medication, and living a structured life. Without structure in the household and structure for the one living with bipolar disorder, this can be detrimental for them and cause a relapse.

Often in a family environment, the person with the illness is dependent on the schedule of others in the household. Therefore, you and the members of the household should create an acceptable schedule that works for all members of the family. For example, if your teenage son occasionally has friends over into the wee hours of the morning, you should consider moving that exercise to another location or set a curfew that is early in the evening for such events.

Setting Boundaries

Setting boundaries for behavior is a great way to avoid conflict. Language and behavior that you refuse to tolerate should be expressed by you as the caregiver, but respect that the bipolar person needs the same courtesy. By defining your expectations, situations can be tolerated much better than by not knowing where the limits are. As well, setting boundaries allows the parties to settle their thoughts and not have to be on constant guard or wonder how much more is considered to be acceptable behavior. There is less confusion because everyone should understand the boundaries, and it allows for independence as each individual understands what is or is not acceptable.

Only set realistic boundaries that are comfortable and easily understood by you and your family. Unrealistic boundaries are pointless. Once the boundaries have been established, you as the caregiver need to be tough to ensure compliance because the boundaries will probably be challenged. Someone with a mood disorder may test your limits, but you must stand firm. Also, someone in the household may test the limits of the person who is ill. Understanding the boundaries will enable the person with bipolar disorder to make sound behavioral choices during recovery from an episode.

You must lead the effort to set the boundaries. We suggest that you begin by identifying the behaviors that you find unacceptable to you, the person with the mood disorder, and the other members of the household. Do not focus on the little stuff, it is not worth it. As the caregiver, you are the one who has to set the limits and be the one who makes the rational and not emotional decisions that will help to keep the person with bipolar disorder on the right track and avoid relapses.

Unacceptable behaviors may include bringing alcohol and drugs into the house or consuming them anywhere. Taunting or making deprecating statements, aggressive or violent behavior, and physical and verbal abuse should all be considered. A noisy environment is detrimental to the patient when depressed or manic, so noise-avoidance boundaries are appropriate. Also, the number of guests in the house at any one time can be limited to minimize the bustle and chaos of everyday life. Nagging attitudes and voice tone can easily be misinterpreted and should be avoided. You will be the most familiar with your family and friends, and you will be able to identify the behaviors that will be unacceptable.

When establishing these unacceptable behaviors, you must set some type of consequence if someone ignores the boundaries that are set. Be sure to establish appropriate consequences and not ones that are overly punitive or demeaning to the individual.

You must enforce the boundaries consistently. Without consistency, your boundaries will become threats and nothing more.

Step Off and Step In
The stress of caring for the bipolar patient that, on occasion, will be a 24-hour-a-day vigil can leave you drained and in need of rest and relaxation. When the cycle stabilizes, that is the time for you to *step off* and *step in* to someplace special for you. That special place is yours. It is a place for you to relax, recharge, and reacquaint yourself with the outside world. Spend time with friends, get away for a couple of days to a favorite place, or just find time for yourself. It is a good idea for the person with the illness to do the same. They may need some reassurance to do this as they have just been through a difficult time, but make it easy for them. Offer to contact their friends or have a mutual friend do it. Either way, know when

it is best for you to step off the caregiver podium and take a break.

If Children are in the Household
Children are a precious gift to us all. As parents, stepparents, or guardians, we are in charge of their lives and this means that you must protect them psychologically from the fallout of the mood disorder.

As a child grows, so too does their brain and their learned behavior of how to react to specific situations. A child's world revolves around them. Children are self-centered (as all healthy children are during brain development/growth) and they will blame themselves for any issues that may arise with their parents or elder siblings.

Reflect for a moment back to your childhood. Do you remember a time when you blamed yourself for a parent's issue? Sure you do, we all did. Imagine for a moment that your father or mother laid in bed all day, would not come out, or spend any time with you. Maybe they would cry at the drop of a hat, scream at you for virtually nothing, or what if you heard them constantly fighting?

This is very difficult for a child because they do not comprehend what we do as adults, nor should you expect them to. Do not take away a childhood or try to make them grow up too fast. A child needs nurturing and self-assurance with consistent positive reinforcement. A child needs to feel secure. You cannot talk to a child as you would an adult. You have to use age-appropriate language and words they understand. If you use the words "mood disorder" or "bipolar", do you think they will understand? Of course not, so use phrases like, "Mommy sometimes is sick and can't get out of bed, like when you have a cold" or "Dad's not doing so well, he's feeling blue or sad, remember when you felt sad..." Make sure to explain the whole disease to them and let them know that the person is okay, especially because of medicines they take. Do not leave anything to question. Give the child time to absorb this information and allow them to ask questions, and make them feel important. If Dad is in bed all day, have the child(ren) make a drawing or some other type of project. Keep them busy and productive; make them feel as if they are helping too. Ask them to help you with the chores. A child's sense of well-being starts with you as the caregiver/parent.

7. Crisis Management

Throughout the patient's life, you will be confronted with episodes of depression and mania. You will not know precisely when they will occur, but if you are vigilant, you will recognize the signs and symptoms that foretell an impending episode. Being proactive will help you to cope better. However, there will be times when the mania and depression will manifest fully and you need to be prepared for the consequences. The patient will need your help and they may need it urgently to prevent them from harming themselves or others. Treat these times as a crisis and be prepared with good crisis management so that you can respond effectively and in a timely manner to meet the patient's needs.

There are characteristic behaviors that the bipolar person may exhibit. In a manic episode, these behaviors may include hypersexuality, drug or alcohol abuse, runaway spending or compulsive shopping, not sleeping for days, threat of suicide, or a myriad of other possible behaviors. On the other hand, your patient may dive into depression. Each individual is different. You may not see any of these behaviors or you could see all of them. Since you will not know precisely what to expect, you and your support team must be ready at all times.

You must plan to respond to the crisis. You should develop a crisis-prevention and intervention plan. If a mood cycle occurs, it is not the time to be asking questions. It is already too late and you must be prepared to act. At this point in time, blaming is not acceptable either and certainly trying to find the cause of the cycle is not relevant.

Time to Make the Crisis-Prevention Plan

When preparing the crisis-prevention and intervention plan, you should involve the patient and the support team consisting of the medical team and trustworthy family members and friends. First, start with the patient to learn what they want you to do. You will find a time to talk to them when they are nonsymptomatic, i.e., they are not depressed or manic. It is advisable to have a third party present who is trusted by you and the patient, and who can lend support and help to keep the conversation going and the ideas flowing. The third party could be the patient's therapist. If they do not have a therapist, you need to consider getting one because therapy is a vital part of treatment for the bipolar I and sometimes the bipolar II patient. If that is not a possibility, consider asking a friend or unbiased third party to help you.

When you talk, it is not a time to place blame, vent anger, or be overly emotional. The discussion you will have may be painful as you bring up experiences of previous episodes, but be supportive and reassure the person that this time of questions and answers will ultimately help them, you, and members of your household to cope during mood cycling.

For your discussion, find a quiet and comfortable place with no distractions. This could be in your home or in the therapist's office. If there are children in the house, find someone to watch them. When having this discussion, you will be establishing the roles and responsibilities for yourself and the support team, and you should keep cool and collected and focus on the planning. Bring a notebook; this is where you will keep all relevant information that you will need in the crisis. Write so others can read your notes.

Work with your patient to compile the following information. You can use this as your checklist:

Health Care Contact Information
(You will need the name, phone number, emergency phone number, and address.)

o Psychiatrist
o Therapist
o Primary care provider
o Local hospital
o Mental health emergency line
o Mental health hospital
o Support group
o Friend/relatives emergency contacts
o Medication log (you will need the name, dose, and times per day – you find this information on the label of the bottle)
o Insurance information
  ▪ Insurance company name
  ▪ Address
  ▪ Group number
  ▪ Policy number (or member ID)

Additional information you will need:

o Employer or school name, address, phone numbers, and human resource or school councilor's contacts
o Bank and credit card account information that includes names of the institutions, phone numbers, and addresses

It is very important that you get the bipolar person's permission in writing to allow you to contact their physician, therapist, school, or work. Have them sign the document; in fact, let them write the whole document. Reassure them that you will use the document only in a time of crisis when they are unable to make rational and prudent decisions. They can write this restriction into the document if it makes them feel more comfortable.

As well as being recognized as a caregiver, you will need to discuss and obtain Power of Attorney. Having Power of Attorney will legally allow you to make decisions for the person you are caring for in the event they are incapacitated by their illness (see Chapter 4).

When you have finished compiling this information, you will need to make several copies to keep at home, in the car, on your person, or PDA. Update the information as needed and make sure the person that you are caring for has this information in their wallet as well. This is confidential information and you must make sure that only those directly involved in caring for your patient have access to it. Financial information should be restricted to only those people who have been given permission by the patient to access it.

The Mood Intervention Team (MIT)
The MIT is an integral part of the support team alongside you and the medical team. You will not always be available to help the patient, so you will need support from others. They will also be there to help you when you need support for yourself.

The first step is to identify the members of your MIT. They should be people that you trust and that are very close to you. They need to be fully educated on the disease and it is advisable for them to use this book, as you are using it, as their guide for continuity of care. They should be briefed and they should receive a copy of the crisis plan that includes them and their roles in managing a crisis.

You will be the coach, cheerleader, case worker, support team, referral service, medication monitor, and the transportation service. With the patient, you must define the roles and responsibilities for you and the MIT. Through discussion, you will identify the reasonable levels of involvement for you and the MIT. All concerned must communicate what role and responsibility they are comfortable with and it must be agreed how to handle sensitive personal issues, such as contacting employers, doctors, or managing assets. Discuss and try to reach agreement on everything. Never assume, as assumption only leads to trouble. Be clear about who is comfortable in certain situations during a crisis and when. If anyone cannot assist the person in a crisis, you need to make that clear and have someone else step in.

The following are the key areas to be included in the crisis-prevention and intervention plan.

Accessibility
Identify who is the most accessible and immediately available in a crisis. You should identify emergency child care, time and distance it will take to get home, human resources to be notified if you have a very ill relative (you do not need to disclose the disease), and who has access to medications. It may be wise to have the main team members of the MIT carry the person's medications for one day in a marked pill bottle in case they are needed.

Roles and Responsibilities
You need to ask questions such as, "How involved will I be?" This is very dependent on your knowledge of everyday management of caregiving. You may be the one who has the best grasp on identifying mood changes or know what behaviors have begun, such as consumption of alcohol and drugs, missed medications, or a personal crisis in that person's life. Will you pull the car keys and credit cards during a mood episode? As well, when is enough, enough? When is your involvement not effective any longer? At what point will you decide to call the person's therapist, psychiatrist, or doctor?

When to Intervene
There will be an insertion point during a crisis that the MIT will drop into. Determining this point can be difficult to identify, but a decision will have to be made. Because a person

is happy does not mean they are manic. You have read about specific signs and symptoms of mania earlier in this book. Saying a person is manic when they are just very happy does not mean, "Hit the panic button, full steam ahead!" Through the use of mood tracking, you will be able to identify the warning signs of an impending mood cycle. If you can identify true warning signs early enough, you need to insert yourself and act. By making this plan, you have created an element of open communication with the person you are caring for and the person will hopefully be more receptive to your observations and suggestions. It is best to set a "key phrase" in the boundaries. The key phrase(s) will identify behaviors, e.g., using the words blue, down, overly excited, not sleeping, tired, etc. Use descriptive words that do not make the person feel as if they are at fault. When making an observation about behavior, remember what we discussed previously, i.e., do not make blame-oriented statements starting with "you", have a softer approach. As an example, "Bob, I've noticed you're a bit blue, what can I do to help?" By setting up the boundary and the "key phrase" in your plan, this will aid the person in acceptance of a manic, hypomanic, or depressive episode so they can contact their clinician and receive treatment.

The nature of a mood cycle is to gain momentum so you should be prepared for resistance. You need to err on the side of caution and know the fine line between pushing too much, hurting the person's feelings, and management of the disease. It is worth the risk of anger if it affects their safety and well-being. If the person will not listen, call for help, but know *when* to call for help. We discuss this later in this chapter. Discuss what you should do for the person if that occurs. This is part of your role and responsibility.

As part of this plan, you need to outline the importance of mood tracking and journaling. The therapist should have a mood chart available for use, but if they do not, refer to about.com's website on bipolar at http://bipolar.about.com/cs/

moodcharting/index.htm. By mood charting, you can track a potential for mood cycling and be able to identify the red flags as they pop up. You can then respond accordingly.

Calling for Help
When red flags begin to fly and the pattern of mood cycling is developing, you may decide together to call the ill person's psychiatrist or therapist. This will be the best solution and it is the time where a description of the situation is to be discussed. If the person is unable to make the call to their therapist, you will make the call. Giving a heads up to the clinicians can help to minimize a mood cycle or prevent it in its entirety with medication or therapy.

If the situation becomes unsafe for you or the person with bipolar disorder, someone else has to step in. You can contact your local Mental Health Crisis Team (find information in your local yellow pages) if the clinicians are not responding to your calls. As well, if the person is cooperative, you can take them to an emergency room. You will need to discuss with the psychiatrist if there is a preference of facilities. This preference may be that you have a predetermined psychiatric hospital or emergency room; ask the doctor, be specific in your plan, and define the doctor's protocol.

If there is danger to life or personal safety, you must call 911. You will do this absolutely in the cases shown below, and there is no compromise. As you have learned earlier in this book, threats of suicide are acted on by those with bipolar disorder and all threats of suicide are to be taken seriously. Do not think someone will not do it or they are just calling out for help. This is a situation a doctor must deal with, not you as the caregiver. You will call 911 when the person threatens to:

o   Commit suicide
o   Act out violently towards others
o   Hit, grab, slap, or use objects to hurt another person

- o Make violent threats
- o Drive dangerously and recklessly
- o Refuse to cooperate with your efforts to help
- o Seclude themselves and refuse to eat

No matter if you feel hurt, discouraged, that you are failing, or that you are not doing the right thing — stop. You are performing the task of a caregiver and performing the acts that best represent the help needed to stabilize the individual with bipolar disorder. If you are to call 911, you must also place a call to the psychiatrist/therapist and notify them of the circumstances and situation.

If you find yourself in this position, you may be facing what is termed a "5150". A "5150" is a medical term or code used by clinicians, hospitals, law enforcement, and fire departments to place a person on an involuntary hospitalization for up to 72 hours for observation. You may face this issue at some point, but it only occurs in specific situations and that includes several of the situations in the previous list and particularly if the person is a threat to self or others.

Each state has its own set of rules for "5150" so you will have to find out what is the process in your state. If the person is to be admitted for a longer hospital stay and involuntarily medicated, a court hearing may or may not have to be held based on your Power of Attorney.

High-Risk Behaviors
High-risk behaviors include illicit drug use and consuming too much alcohol, hypersexuality, runaway spending, reckless driving, and criminal activity, all of which are potentially life-threatening activities.

Drug and alcohol abuse are common symptoms in bipolar disorder. As soon as this is recognized, you must inform the medical team so that the alcohol and drug abuse can be treated at the same time as the bipolar disorder.

Hypersexuality not only includes the hurt and betrayal to wedding vows or relationship promises, but there is also a risk of acquiring a sexually transmitted disease such as herpes, Chlamydia, syphilis, or human immunodeficiency virus (HIV). The more sexual partners someone has, the more the risk. Because they lack judgment at this point, the bipolar person may not use protection, such as a male or female condom.

Uncontrolled spending is a common symptom of a manic episode. The bipolar person can easily clean out bank accounts to which they have access and run up charges on credit cards. Now that you are aware of this problem, you can do something to put controls in place to curb the spending. Agree with your patient to set low limits on their credit cards and limit the number of credit cards to which they have access. Limit their access to your bank account such as dual signature checks, limit the debit cards, and control access to the online banking. This may sound like you are taking the person hostage, but by doing this you will avoid bigger financial problems.

If you are unable to take these steps or you cannot reach agreement, or if the patient has nothing to do with your accounts, you should try to reach agreement that, during mood cycles, access to computers will be limited, holds will be placed on credit/debit cards, and access to telephone purchases will be limited. You can also limit the amount of money in the person's personal bank account. These steps may be difficult to implement because your patient will need access to their money and accounts when they are symptom free. However, try to reach a compromise that works best for all concerned.

Reckless driving is often a problem incurred as both mania and depression impair a person's motor functions and create difficulty in reaction time when driving. This is not only dangerous to the bipolar person, but to their passengers and other drivers on the road as well. Driving is a sign of independence and taking away a person's right to drive is not something that can be done lightly. However, there needs to be some recognition of the dangers, since mania can cause a person to drive recklessly by ignoring speed limits and forgetting about rules of the road. On the other side of the coin, depression causes slowed motor reaction and impaired concentration. Therefore, you must agree that there is to be no driving during mood cycling, the keys are handed over and hidden, and a plan to help the person with transportation is needed. You will need to arrange for someone to drive them to doctor's appointments, work, school, or functions. They should not be isolated because you planned poorly or you or the MIT are unwilling to drive them. You must offer a solution. Ask friends, relatives, or find a transportation service (whether private or public) that they can utilize. Either way, you need to agree on a plan to provide transportation.

Crimes may be committed by those with impaired judgment and the bipolar patient is in this category. You or the MIT will have to be there to be that person's advocate if the person is arrested. As the advocate, you will identify to the police that this individual has a mental illness called bipolar disorder that impairs judgment and you will ask for a "5150" or involuntary commitment to a hospital for treatment. You will need to notify the person's physician, psychiatrist, therapist, and lawyer. The clinicians may be able to speak with the police to help facilitate this request for treatment. Jail is not the prudent institution for someone with bipolar disorder. You must strive to get them hospitalized.

Once the crisis-prevention and intervention plan has been completed, make sure that everyone concerned has a copy, including the patient, and review with the MIT their roles and responsibilities. Stay in touch with the MIT and remind them constantly what is expected of them. Your role as coach works for the patient and the MIT. They will all look to you for leadership in the time of crisis. Thorough preparation that involves everyone directly involved in the management of the crisis, so they know what to expect and what they should do, will go a long way to helping your patient in their time of need.

8. Caring for Your Bipolar Child and Adolescent

In previous chapters, we described the diagnosis, symptoms, and treatments for bipolar children and adolescents. We provided you with suggestions as to how to interact with your medical team and described the planning you should undertake. In another chapter, we provided information on how to put your own support group together. Now, we will consider the issues you will face while caring for your bipolar child or adolescent, and some of the things you can do to make it possible for them to live as normal a life as their disease permits.

First, you must manage your own emotions and reactions after learning that your child has bipolar disorder. You will find yourself facing a whole range of emotions including guilt, anger, and sadness over your child's diagnosis. You must accept that your child has this disease, get over any stigma or embarrassment that your child has a mental illness, and educate those around you to understand bipolar disorder and what it means to your family and friends. Speaking openly about bipolar disorder and the available treatments will help you to be emotionally fit to take care of your child.

If you are a parent who also has bipolar disorder, you will be aware of the stigma associated with this disease, but do not let any of your own bad experiences get in the way of doing the right things for your child. If you had good experiences, you can share them to help relieve the child's fear and apprehension about the future. Your job as a parent is to make sure that your child has the opportunity for a healthy start in life and that means sometimes making personally painful or difficult decisions. Remember, this is not about you.

If you have bipolar disorder yourself, you must have your own support team in place that can communicate with your child and their support team when episodes occur.

Your child is facing a lifetime of illness management and you want to be able to instill good habits in them to follow their plan of medication and other therapy, to recognize the signs of impending episodes of depression and mania, and to have confidence that they will receive prompt and effective support from you, family members, friends, and their medical team. They should have confidence that when they call, someone will be there to help.

It is important for everyone involved with treating and supporting your child that there is no fault implied, nobody is to blame. Your child is not sick because you did something wrong or you are a bad parent, nor did they ask for this disease. It is something that happened to them. Your approach of empathy, loving support, setting boundaries/consequences, and vigilance to keep order is vital to their well-being.

Education for the Bipolar Child and Adolescent
There are few things more damaging to the development of any child than losing their education, from preschool through high school and beyond. To have a rewarding life in today's society, it is essential for children to be educated to the levels demanded by employers. The bipolar child who may not have been diagnosed, who is not receiving the correct medications or level of care, or who is not in a responsive school system is at a huge disadvantage. Once again, it is crucial that as soon as you suspect symptoms, your child must see a qualified physician to receive a diagnosis. Once diagnosed, you must make sure that your child receives a proper education in an environment that understands your child's needs. The bipolar

child has rights under the law and it is your responsibility as the parent/caregiver to make sure that they receive their due.

In 1997, the United States Congress amended and updated the Individuals with Disabilities in Education Act (IDEA) that mandates, under certain circumstances, that children with disabilities have the right to the same education as other healthy children. Your child is disabled by a neurochemical imbalance that affects mood and behavior that may prevent them from being in a regular classroom atmosphere. Your child may have special needs and, just like any child that has special needs, the school system has specialized education services to help educate your child.

In order to access the services under IDEA, you must request a special education evaluation in writing to the director of special education. The school district has 30 school days to respond to your letter. Once they accept your request, your child will have a psychosocial exam and learning ability assessment performed by a social worker or district psychologist. On completion of the exam, an appointment will be set with a team who assesses individualized educational needs and an Individual Education Plan (IEP) meeting will be held. That meeting will determine if your child is eligible for services. Before that meeting occurs, you will need to prepare an education packet. Many school systems do not understand mood disorders and there is a particular lack of understanding about bipolar disorder. The teachers' and administrators' experience with bipolar disorders may be limited, and you will need to educate the educator. You should gather supporting research, data, or information from your child's primary care provider, psychiatrist, or therapist, and bring them to the meeting. You must communicate the basic issues of bipolar disorder and the challenges your child will face with that diagnosis. Come armed with questions about how they will meet your child's specific needs.

The team you will meet with is made up of a special education specialist, your child's teacher, possibly the school's administrator, and you. If you are married, your spouse should attend as well. You are your child's advocate at the meeting because you know your child's needs the best and you understand their behavioral triggers and the challenges they face. The teacher will also give their impressions of your child's needs as well as the special education evaluation that was performed. It is worth mentioning that you should also request that the child's therapist consult with the team to explain their observations and what they believe the child needs in order to be successful in school. You will be required to agree with the IEP by your signature.

If your child is eligible and the IEP is in place, your job is to communicate with the child's teachers on a daily or weekly basis to keep abreast of how your child is performing and to provide your feedback on how the child is performing based on what you see and hear at home and in their social life. You will also encourage communication between the teacher and your child's therapist or psychiatrist as this is relevant in their therapy sessions. Biweekly or weekly reports are most effective for documenting the issues that need to be addressed at therapy. Ask for this request to be placed in the IEP.

If the school decides that your child is *not* disabled (and therefore not eligible) or you fear the word "disabled" personally, both are sorely wrong. Your child *is* disabled. They have a neurochemical imbalance that prevents them from making rational decisions, from having stable and predictable moods, and they have limited ability to organize or focus for long periods of time during a mood episode.

If your IEP meeting ends with a rejection and your pleas for inclusion do not work, turn to the Rehabilitation Act of 1973 and American with Disabilities Act, section 504. This specific section of the Act requires all school systems to provide a modified education for a child with a disability. This Act was designed to prevent school systems from discriminating against any child with a disability and offer them the same education as the nondisabled child. These services do not require the IEP as this is specifically for needs of less severity. In other words, it cuts out a lot of red tape for the school. Your child needs these services and you can use Section 504 of the aforementioned Act to achieve this goal. Section 504 mandates that a school district will provide educational modifications based on a child's unique needs. For example, these include separate testing areas and extended time limits for taking a test, they may take oral tests rather than written ones, and many other services. Each district will have its own procedures for obtaining these services and they vary from school district to district as do the services provided. We suggest that you have your child's clinicians write a letter stating that they have specific learning needs under section 504 of the Rehabilitation Act of 1973.

You must be persistent and insistent to make sure that the school provides the special services your child will need. By taking care of this, your child will be able to overcome many of the educational disadvantages they would otherwise face and they will be able to prosper in a stable learning environment. Combine that with regular therapy, compliance with medication, organization, a healthy lifestyle, and a supportive loving home environment and you have an opportunity to create the needed skills for your son or daughter to have a successful transition to adulthood and a stable life.

Compliance with Therapy
Bipolar disorder is treatable, and with the medications and therapy prescribed by the psychiatrist or primary care provider, your child's symptoms can be managed and the child can lead a relatively normal life. You can expect relapses,

even when they are taking their medications, but episodes will be less frequent when their therapeutic regimen is followed.

Keep in mind that depressive episodes are the most common and when your child comes out of an episode, they will inevitably feel better. This is a danger period because when they feel better, they will be tempted not to take their medication or show up for a therapy session. You must be strict with them, monitor them carefully, and make sure that they continue to take their medications and go to therapy no matter how much they resist you.

We cannot emphasize enough the importance of compliance with therapy and it is your responsibility to make sure that the regimen is followed rigorously. Be vigilant for signs and symptoms of impending episodes and keep track of the perceived (by you and your child) effectiveness and side effects of the medications. If you find that the medications do not seem as effective or if side effects seem worse, consult your primary care provider or psychiatrist immediately.

How to Manage the Behaviors You Should Expect
Whatever behavior is exhibited during a bipolar episode, do not take the behavior personally. The child has little control over their moods and behavior as a result of their illness, and it is certainly not directed at you no matter how much it appears that way. Do not shame or blame your child for his or her behavior as you will only make things worse and damage their self-esteem. They did not ask for this disease. Blame impairs your ability to parent effectively. Your child is in distress. Staying calm and supportive is the prudent course to follow.

If your son or daughter comes to you to discuss how they feel, do not minimize their emotion. Be there and have empathy. All they want is for you to listen about the emotional challenges they are facing. Commonly, a parent faces a child's need to fit in with his or her peers. For a bipolar child, they will focus on how different they are. Reassure them that they are alright, but do not be dismissive. This is a normal childhood feeling. If you have trouble coping with the moods and behaviors, remember that you are not alone. Use the medical team and support team, and find a solution.

Children and adolescents are dramatic, moody, and impulsive by nature. They know it all and they consider themselves invincible. Often when a child is depressed or has an illness, they will act as if nothing is wrong. For fear of embarrassment, they will hide their sadness and do what any person does, i.e., try to make themselves feel better. So how can you tell the difference between a healthy child and a bipolar child? Following are some situations and answers.

Suicide
The leading cause of death in teenagers is suicide. The risk of suicide is raised significantly in the bipolar adolescent, and suicide threats and threats of self-inflicted harm must be taken seriously. Get immediate help from your medical and support teams. Watch for signs. If you notice the child using phrases like, "If I'm gone...", "When I go...", or "When I'm gone..." you should be alerted. They may not directly say that they are going to commit suicide, but other subtle messages may include talking about hopelessness, how sad they are, or that they are filled with despair. Also, if you see them quickly or suddenly pulling back from activities they enjoy, or they are preparing to or are giving away personal effects, these are signs. Be aware of other signs, such as substance abuse, that may give an indication of a worsening of their condition and impending harmful activities. If you have concerns about your child's desire to commit suicide, do not be afraid to bring it up. Your question will not create the child's desire to kill themselves, but not asking or your lack of attention could help provide a ripe environment for that opportunity.

If you believe that your child is contemplating suicide, you need to speak with their clinicians. The doctor or therapist may recommend or admit the child to the hospital for care and observation for a short period of time for crisis management and stabilization of your child's mood and behavior. Psychiatric hospitalization is not long term unless the person is unable to care for themselves or is a permanent threat to others or themselves. There is no shame in psychiatric help. Your job is to ensure their safety and well-being.

You should always be prepared for a potential hospitalization. You should start by speaking with the child's therapist and psychiatrist, and you should ask them for a game plan in the event of attempted suicide or out-of-control behavior. Ask the clinicians for their choices of hospitals and compare the list to the one listed with your insurance coverage. Pick the one under your plan that is most convenient to you and your doctors.

The psychiatric hospital under your HMO or PPO may not be a facility where your child's doctor has privileges. In this situation, you must make sure that there is a complete exchange of information between yourself, your doctors, and the attending physician (the doctor who is treating your child at the hospital).

If your child is in the hospital, the staff may use PRN medications, which means "as needed". These medications could be chemical restraints that are used to subdue the patient and make them more controllable. For the patient who is out-of-control, it may be necessary to use physical restraints. You need to be aware of the hospital's policies and you must insist that you are contacted if they find that either of these strategies is needed.

If hospitalization does occur, you will need to be there for your child even if they do not want you there. Being close is very important and you want to make sure the hospital knows you are there and observing. Your child will need you and you will spend many long hours at the hospital. Your crisis plan should have alternates designated to help you with your tasks at home while you are with your child at the hospital.

The safety of your home is something you must also consider. Are there dangerous or sharp objects; other medications; poisonous solutions, such as bleach or pesticides; or any items they could use to harm themselves and others? Make your home a safe place for your child by making sure that potentially dangerous objects are locked away or otherwise unobtainable.

What if my child is withdrawn and distant?
All children and teenagers, in particular, like "their space" so you may find that the child is spending time alone in their room or with their friends. This is normal behavior. However, if you find that the child or teenager is not participating or is slowly withdrawing from weekend activities, time with friends, or after-school functions, you should be concerned. These signs may be gradual and could be a sign of depression, and your child needs your attention and your help. Empathize with the child, approach them on their level, and try to find a way to enter their world and find out what is ailing them. It could be as simple as issues with friends, girl- or boyfriends, family, or school. If you have a family therapist, consult with them on the best course of action. Also, discuss the signs and symptoms with your primary care provider.

Why is my child sleeping a lot?
It is normal for children's sleep patterns to change as they grow older. Teenagers love to stay up late and sleep in. Most parents will remember their own teen years and recognize this behavior. However, if the child's or teen's energy level has dropped, they are sleeping longer, and the symptoms last more than 14 days, you should consult your primary care provider because there

could be a medical issue such as hypothyroidism, vitamin deficiency, or mononucleosis presenting. You should schedule an exam and discuss other signs or symptoms that you have noticed, such as they are very down or too hyper. The more information you can provide, the better it is for the proper diagnosis.

The bipolar child and adolescent exhibits changes in their sleep patterns that you will probably notice. Be vigilant and communicate with your medical team about any unusual or significantly changing sleep patterns or energy loss.

I found out my kid's been doing drugs and drinking.
The use of drugs or alcohol can be a sign of self-medicating for depression or another issue. It is not normal behavior for any person to be high or drunk every weekend or frequently, and this is something you should look into. Talk to your child and consult your family therapist or primary care provider for assistance. Alcohol and drug abuse are symptoms of bipolar disorder and bipolar disorder should be considered if your child is not yet diagnosed. If your child has a bipolar diagnosis and you suspect or know they are abusing drugs or alcohol, immediate intervention is required so the abuse and bipolar disorder can be treated together.

What to do if your child is throwing tantrums and being destructive.
The bipolar child or adolescent will throw tantrums, often destructive, that may harm themselves and others. The child must be restrained to prevent further harm being done, but they must be restrained in a nonviolent way to encourage them to stop. Words of encouragement and empathy in a calming voice will be helpful to get the child to relax. It may be easier to enlist the help of one of your support team if you are managing a large child or adolescent. You can be proactive in your approach by teaching your child relaxation techniques as soon as they recognize the signs of an impending episode.

Relaxation techniques including breathing control, exercises, and massage are all helpful. External stimuli such as music, relaxing sounds (e.g., running water), and lower lighting can also help your child to relax.

9. Support

It is essential for your well-being that you put together a support group to help you when taking care of your patient as well as to provide support for yourself. Support will take different forms depending on your needs at any given time, but certainly you should expect that the need for support will increase with time. Support may come from family and friends; governmental, informal, and specialized organizations; religious groups; and from information sources such as the Internet. It is never too early to start thinking about putting together your support group once you know that you will be the caregiver. It is certainly not too early to inform yourself about this disorder.

Find out which of your family members and friends you can rely on to help you with various tasks, transportation, moral support, conversation partner, etc. Also, make up your own mind as to what degree you think you will be able to rely on them. Some people are simply unreliable — they say the right things and they mean well, but when it comes to crunch time, they are nowhere to be found. These are people you may choose to keep as friends, for conversation, or for a cup of coffee, but you do not want to be in a position of having them let you down when you really need their help and their presence. Do not include these people in your mood intervention team no matter how well you get on with them. Pick out the family members and friends you can count on and talk to them about what you might want them to do. Make sure that they understand the level of support you are expecting from them. Give them the chance to tell you what they can and cannot do, or what they are prepared to do. Keep in mind that you are going to need people that live close by. Also, they have their own lives to lead and their responsibilities to their own families, and there will be times when they will have higher priorities and will not be able to do what you expect. For this reason, you should have as wide a support group as possible to make sure that you have backup when you need it.

In addition to support from family and friends, there are more formal support groups that are there to help you when you need advice based on experience with the bipolar patient. These support groups are often available in your community so make a point to find out what community resources are available in your area. Your psychiatrist, therapist, or primary care provider should be able to help you. If you are a member of a religious organization, they are often able to help either by providing services or advising you about what services are available in your community.

The organized support groups can supply many benefits, such as providing a forum where you can talk to others. Sharing experiences with those in a similar situation can be helpful when dealing with the stress of caregiving and provides an opportunity to:

- Meet new friends and acquaintances
- Learn from others and share with others
  - Experiences with bipolar disorder
  - Available resources in your community
- Express your negative feelings in an environment where you are understood and not criticized
- Receive moral support and encouragement and feel better about yourself
- Get out of the house

There are support groups on the Internet and there is a great deal of information available on the Internet. We have provided some URLs below to help you find the information that you will need. Chat rooms on the Internet can provide a source of information, and the opportunity to share experiences and obtain useful advice from other caregivers, but a word of caution is needed before you heed the advice of unqualified people. Check with your physician before making any changes to the plan of care or to the daily routine.

However, information alone will not be enough; you will need human support from your family and friends and from the organized support groups.

Internet Resources

By no means exhaustive, this list of contact websites will help you to find more information on bipolar disorder and the resources that are available to you. If you have time to browse the Internet, simply typing "bipolar disorder" into your favorite search engine will provide you with a wealth of information.

www.isbd.org/links.htm
www.dbsalliance.org/
www.bpkids.org
www.harbor-of-refuge.org/
www.moodswing.org/supportgroups.html
www.findthelight.net
www.moodgarden.org/forum/
www.walkers.org/
www.bpso.org/
http://draonline.org/index.html
www.nimh.nih.gov/publicat/bipolar.cfm
www.nami.org/Template.cfm?section=Find_Support

10. Scientific and Medical Basis
of Bipolar Disorder

Bipolar disorder is an illness of the brain the cause of which is unknown. However, researchers and clinicians focusing on elucidating the underlying causes of the disease have made some discoveries that are giving clues about the cause of bipolar disorder and giving direction to future avenues of research. These clues indicate a genetic link, neurochemical imbalances, and abnormal brain anatomy in bipolar patients. Before we take a closer look at the research and clinical findings in bipolar disorder, we will present some of the basics of brain anatomy and physiology to make it easier to place the research and clinical findings in context.

The nervous system is made up of two main parts: the central nervous system (CNS) composed of the brain and spinal cord, and the peripheral nervous system. For the purposes of focusing on bipolar disorder, we will only discuss the brain.

The cerebral cortex or cerebrum makes up the largest part of the brain. Its surface has many deep fissures (sulci) and convolutions (gyri), giving it a wrinkled appearance. It has two halves (hemispheres) that are connected by a thick band of nerve fibers. As seen in Figure 1, each half of the cerebrum is made up of four lobes:

1. The occipital lobe, located in the back of the brain, handles visual information.
2. The parietal lobe, lying above the occipital lobe, plays an important role in sorting and interpreting information from the various senses.

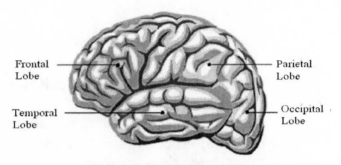

Figure 1: Cerebrum

3. The frontal lobe, as its name suggests, is in the front of the brain. This lobe has functions that include cognitive (complex thinking, language, reasoning, problem solving) and behavioral features (impulse control, judgment, sexual behavior, socialization).
4. The temporal lobe is located beneath the frontal lobe. This lobe functions in hearing, language, and speech, as well as in memory.

The areas of the cerebrum that are currently considered to be involved in bipolar disorder are parts of the frontal lobe and the temporal lobe. These areas are closely linked with a deeper area of the brain, the limbic system, associated with emotion, motivation, emotional association with memory, and mood. The limbic system and associated brain structures have been shown to be altered in their anatomy and in their neurochemical function in patients with bipolar spectrum disorder.

The structures of the limbic system and the areas believed to be associated with bipolar disorder are shown in Figure 2. The roles of some of these structures, as far as they have been discovered, are summarized as follows:

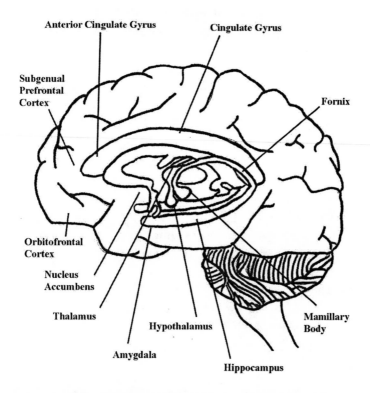

Figure 2. The Limbic System and Associated Structures

- *Amygdala* — The fear and aggression center, the emotional center.
- *Anterior cingulate gyrus* — Increased activity in anterior cingulate is associated with sadness and has been described as the interface between emotion and cognition. It renders new memories permanent.
- *Cingulate gyrus* — Part of the cortex; the limbic cortex, responsible for cognitive and attentional processing as well as for regulating heart rate and blood pressure.
- *Hippocampus* — The long-term memory center.
- *Hypothalamus* — Regulates the sleep/wake cycle as well as hunger, thirst, and sexual arousal. Also

involved in blood pressure and heart rate regulation. Regulates the autonomic nervous system by hormone production and release.

o *Mamillary body* — Involved in memory formation.
o *Nucleus accumbens* — Reward, pleasure, and addiction.
o *Orbitofrontal cortex* — Decision making.
o *Thalamus* — Damage to the thalamus by, for example, a stroke often results in mood swings.

Other Structures:
o *Subgenual prefrontal cortex* — An interface of decision making (prefrontal cortex) and emotional (amygdala) parts of the brain.

Brain Cells
The brain is almost entirely composed of two kinds of cells called neurons and glia. Neurons are the nerve cells and glia are the cells that support the neurons and enable them to function.

Glia (Also Called Neuroglia or Glial Cells)
The glial cells support the neurons (see below) in the brain by providing metabolic support and nutrition, and immune protection; maintaining homeostasis; forming myelin; and participating in signal transmission in the CNS. Glia are unable to generate action potentials or transmit electrical impulses and do not participate in neuronal communication. Unlike neurons, glia can regenerate if injured. Glia affect several processes including regulation of extracellular potassium, glucose storage and metabolism, and glutamate uptake, all of which are crucial for normal neuronal activity. Several different kinds of glia have been identified and their functions are understood:

Astrocytes (also astroglia) are the most numerous of the glial cells and provide structural support to neurons and attach the neurons to their blood supply. They help to regulate and control the external environment of the neurons and play a crucial role in clearing neurotransmitters out of the synaptic cleft (see below). There are two types of astrocytes: protoplasmic astrocytes typically found in grey matter and fibrous astrocytes typically found in white matter.

Microglia are glial cells that do a cleanup job in the brain by removing dead cellular material and bacteria. The microglia have phagocytic capabilities and literally eat up the debris.

Ependymal cells (also ependymocytes) line the ventricles in the brain and have hair-like protrusions called cilia that move to help circulate the cerebrospinal fluid (CSF). A specialized set of ependymal cells called the choroid plexus secretes CSF into the ventricles to maintain the volume of the CSF in the ventricles of the brain and in the spinal cord.

Oligodendrocytes are the cells that coat the axons of the neurons to form the myelin sheath that provides insulation and allows electrical signals to propagate more efficiently. The greater the amount of myelin around an axon, the faster the rate of nerve impulse transmission. Myelinated neurons make up the "white matter" (see below) of the brain and are responsible for information transmission.

Radial glia have different functions depending on the age of the brain. In the developing nervous system, the radial glia provide a support structure on which new neurons can migrate and they are the progenitors of the neurons themselves. In the mature brain, the radial glia have specialized functions in the cerebellum and the retina of the eye.

Neurons

The brain contains millions of neurons. These are the cells that transmit electrical impulses, called action potentials, which enable the brain to communicate with other neurons and all the areas and systems of the body including muscles, organs, eyes, ears, etc. Neurons are able to collect and process information from sources outside and inside the body, and pass on the information to other neurons and other kinds of cells such as muscle cells, thus enabling the body to respond to stimuli. The neurons in the brain are also responsible for extremely complex functions such as memory, reasoning, moods, behavior, language, etc. Neurons are unable to regenerate if they are injured.

The neuron comprises a nerve cell body with two kinds of projections. The projections that transmit information towards the nerve cell body from other neurons are called dendrites. They tend to be short, not myelinated, and numerous. The second kind of projection is called an axon. It transmits nerve signals away from the nerve cell body to other nerves, muscles, etc. Neurons have usually only one axon that tends to be long and may be myelinated (white matter) or not myelinated (grey matter).

The communication between neurons is facilitated by the process known as neurotransmission (see below) that takes place at the nerve endings in a gap or junction between the nerve endings of adjoining cells. This gap is called the synapse and many medications effective in bipolar disorder are active in altering neurotransmission in the synaptic region (see Figure 3).

White Matter

Composed of myelinated axons, white matter connects the various grey matter areas of the brain to each other and carries nerve impulses between neurons. The axons tend to be grouped together in bundles that conduct specific information such as pain or touch. Cerebral and spinal cord white matter do not contain dendrites. White matter is generally considered to be responsible for information transmission, a process that is made more efficient and faster by the myelin sheath.

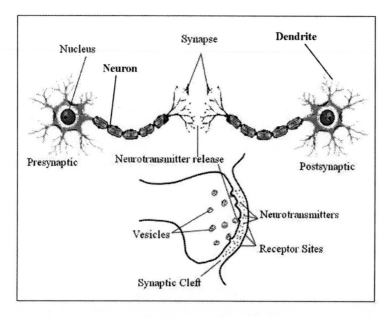

Figure 3: Neuron and Synapse

<u>Grey Matter</u>
Actually pinkish in color, grey matter contains many nerve cell bodies, processes (axons and dendrites) that are not myelinated, a few myelinated axons, and is responsible primarily for information processing. This is where the nerve impulses for many of our mental functions originate, which are then carried to their targets by the white matter. In areas of the brain that have a specialized function such as memory or speech, nerve cell bodies tend to cluster together to form nuclei (not to be confused with the nucleus inside the cell). Examples of these nuclei include the caudate nuclei, thalami, raphe nuclei, and putamen.

Neurotransmission
Researchers have detected changes in the biochemical functioning of the brain in patients with bipolar disorder and it is well established that many of the medications effective in treating bipolar disorder act by modifying the neurochemical balance in specific areas of the brain. To understand these changes, it helps to understand the process of neurotransmission.

As we noted above, neurons transmit action potentials (small electrical charges). These action potentials cause neurons to release chemicals (neurotransmitters) that move between nerve cells across the synapse. This is illustrated in Figure 3. When a neurotransmitter is released from a nerve ending, some of the neurotransmitter interacts with receptors on the nerve endings of the postsynaptic cell to elicit a response from that cell. Excess neurotransmitter is either broken down by enzymes (monoamine oxidase breaks down serotonin and norepinephrine) or is taken back up into the presynaptic nerve ending in a process called reuptake. From the chapter on therapies you may recognize how drugs work in the brain by their names. For example, SSRIs are serotonin reuptake inhibitors and MAOIs are monoamine oxidase inhibitors, and the result of both of these classes of drugs is to increase the amount of neurotransmitter in the synaptic cleft, resulting in increased neurotransmitter activity that elicits a greater response from the postsynaptic cell.

Neurotransmitters
Neurotransmitters are the chemicals that neurons use to transmit messages to one another and to the rest of the body. After the chemicals are released from the neurons, they travel across the synapses and bind to receptors on nearby cells and stimulate those cells to respond. There are several types of neurotransmitters in the brain, each has differing functions. Some are excitatory (causing nerve stimulation), whereas others are inhibitory (inhibiting nerve stimulation).

Glutamate is the most common excitatory neurotransmitter in the brain. Studies have identified glutamate as being critical in the formation of memory as well as the generation of new connections between neurons. Glutamate triggers the receptors on a target nerve cell, called N-methyl-D-aspartate (NMDA) receptors, to allow the right amount of calcium to flow in the nerve cell. This is necessary for nerve cells to function normally and, in particular, to store information. Without enough glutamate, the chemical environment for successful transmission and formation of memory is not created and information cannot be stored. On the other hand, too much glutamate or calcium can damage nerve cells.

Acetylcholine is another type of excitatory neurotransmitter. It functions both within the brain and throughout the body. In the brain, it is important in cognition and memory. In the body, it controls salivation, heart rate, sweating, and muscle movements. Acetylcholine is quickly removed from the synapse by a special enzyme called acetylcholinesterase that breaks it down to its original chemical components. These components are not active and are then recycled to make more acetylcholine. Another enzyme like acetylcholinesterase is called butyrylcholinesterase. This enzyme also aids in the breakdown of acetylcholine.

Serotonin (5-hydroxytryptamine) is a neurotransmitter that is believed to play a significant role in depression and bipolar disorder. Indeed, there seems to be a link between serotonin dysfunction and suicidal behavior. Drugs such as SSRIs and MAOIs that are effective in reducing the symptoms of bipolar disorder have been shown to be active in raising the levels of serotonin in the brain. Serotonergic neurons are closely located to norepinephrine-containing neurons and the two seem to work in conjunction in the limbic system.

Norepinephrine (noradrenaline) is another neurotransmitter in the brain that may be involved in the symptomology of bipolar disorder. The noradrenergic system is active in the awake state and seems to be important for focused attention. A brain area called the locus ceruleus that appears to be involved in pleasure and anxiety contains many noradrenergic neurons. The turnover of brain norepinephrine increases in times of stress. Antianxiety drugs such as benzodiazepines (Valium, etc.) decrease neuronal firing in the locus ceruleus, thereby reducing the amount of norepinephrine distributed to the amygdala and forebrain, areas involved in bipolar disorder. Increasing the levels of norepinephrine by using drugs such as tricyclic antidepressants or drugs that affect serotonergic (and maybe dopaminergic) neurons as well (SNRIs [see Glossary], MAOIs) alleviate the symptoms of depression.

Dopamine is another neurotransmitter that may be involved in bipolar disorder. Dopamine is closely related to norepinephrine chemically and exists in distinct dopaminergic neurons in the brain. Dopamine and norepinephrine are both members of the class of compounds called catecholamines. Dopamine is associated with several functions in the brain including controlling movement, prolactin secretion, and in pleasure and motivation. Dopamine disorders in the frontal lobes of the cerebrum can cause a decline in cognitive functions, memory, attention, and problem solving, and reduced levels of dopamine in the prefrontal cortex may be associated with ADHD and other disorders. Also, the dopaminergic system is strongly linked with psychosis because drugs that specifically block dopamine receptors (specifically the receptors described as D2) reduce psychotic symptoms.

Genetics and Bipolar Disorder
The fact that bipolar disorder runs in families has been extensively documented and a genetic cause for bipolar disorder is well accepted. However, bipolar disorder is not considered a single disorder and no single gene that causes bipolar disorder has been found. Rather, we talk about the

bipolar spectrum, a whole range of disorders, and researchers have identified many genes that could be implicated in the bipolar spectrum.

Researchers use a technique called linkage analysis to try to find the genes associated with diseases of unknown origin such as bipolar disorder. They compare the DNA of families with a history of bipolar disorder to known genome maps from, for example, the Human Genome Project, and try to find the areas that might code for bipolar disorder. This technique has been successful in elucidating the genes associated with schizophrenia and it is hoped that future research will identify the genes associated with bipolar spectrum disorder. Once these genes are known, we will have a better understanding of the underlying causes of bipolar disorder and the hope is that this will, in turn, lead to more effective therapies.

As mentioned in an earlier chapter, even though bipolar disorder is inherited, not all children will show the symptoms. In families with one parent with bipolar disorder, the chance of a child inheriting the disease is 15–30%, while if both parents have the disease, the chance increases to 50–75%. Bipolar disorder can skip generations and can manifest in different forms within the bipolar spectrum, i.e., if the parent has bipolar I, it does not mean that the child will also have bipolar I.

Just as it is now obvious that bipolar is an inherited disease, it is just as obvious that it is triggered by an event, an environmental factor, such as trauma, stress, or drug abuse. How the environmental factors interact with the multiple genes that may be involved in bipolar disorder is not known. Some researchers have suggested that excess glutamate in the brain caused by the secretion of cortisol that is released by the body in response to stressful stimuli may be the cause. Patients with bipolar disorder may be unable to clear out the excess glutamate because it has been shown that in some areas of the brain (see below), they have fewer glial cells than normal and the glia are responsible for getting rid of the excess glutamate.

So why are the genes important and how do they work? Genes themselves do not necessarily determine that an individual will get a particular disease. The genes are responsible for making the proteins that are responsible for the structure and function of cells. As long as the genes work normally, the cells and organs of the body should work normally. However, if there is an error in the coding of a gene, the resultant proteins may alter the normal structure and function of the cell resulting in a pathology or disease.

Brain Abnormalities in Bipolar Disorder

Research studies have tried to discover whether abnormalities in neurodevelopment, neurodegeneration, or both, play a major role in the pathophysiology of bipolar spectrum disorder. Unfortunately, there is no clear answer to the question, but it has been suggested that these processes could act together. Neuronal and glial loss that occurs during childhood and adolescence may be responsible for the onset of bipolar disorder, while subsequent neurotoxic mechanisms and impaired ability for regrowth or damage repair and cellular resilience may be responsible for further disease progression.

Anatomical Changes

There are several techniques available that allow researchers and clinicians to see the living brain as it functions without the need for surgery. These imaging techniques include magnetic resonance imaging (MRI), functional magnetic resonance imaging (fMRI), and positron emission tomography (PET). Several interesting features have been discovered, indicating that the brains of bipolar patients differ anatomically from the brains of healthy people and the level of neuronal activity may also differ. The brain areas that seem to be involved in bipolar disorder include the amygdala, basal ganglia, subgenual prefrontal cortex, anterior cingulate, dorsolateralprefrontal cortex, superior temporal gyrus, striatum, corpus collosum, and hippocampus. White matter hyperintensities, which are nonspecific abnormalities, are also common in bipolar patients. Cortical volume is also smaller in bipolar patients.

Bipolar patients may lose more brain grey matter by aging. There is also evidence for impaired myelination of the corpus collosum in bipolar disorder. Lithium may reverse or prevent grey matter prefrontal cortex abnormalities in bipolar patients by its neuroprotective effects.

While not all research studies are in agreement, the subgenual region of the anterior cingulate has been identified in several studies as being reduced in size in bipolar patients and may play a role in the disease. Also, the number of glia associated with the neurons in this area was found to be markedly reduced in bipolar patients.

The subgenual prefrontal cortex is an area where the neuronal impulses from the amygdala (the emotional center) and the prefrontal cortex (a decision-making center) meet. The communication that takes place in the subgenual region determines the eventual response of the person, and their emotions and emotional behaviors are regulated in this area. Serotonin receptors of two types, one excitatory and the other inhibitory, seem to be responsible for maintaining a balance. It is conceivable that altered functionality or reduced size or number of glia that have been found in the subgenual area could be responsible, at least in part, for altering mood.

Smaller volume of the hippocampus has also been reported in bipolar patients so this too may be involved in the pathophysiology of the disease.

Pathophysiology of Bipolar Disorder
The functional changes associated with or resulting from bipolar disorder are not completely understood, although

evidence tends to support the view that the symptoms of bipolar disorder are the result of abnormalities in brain biochemistry, particularly imbalances in one or more of the neurotransmitters associated with the areas of the brain responsible for mood and emotions. Neurotransmitter imbalances have been detected in neurons containing serotonin, norepinephrine, dopamine, and glutamate. Abnormalities have also been detected in other chemicals involved in cell metabolism. It has also been suggested that mitochondrial dysfunction resulting in an overall decrease in energy production may also play a role in bipolar disorder. Mitochondria are the power plants of the cell, producing energy for normal cellular functioning.

Furthermore, abnormalities of the hypothalamic-pituitary-adrenal (HPA) axis may play a part in bipolar disorder. Under normal conditions, cortisol levels are raised in the body in times of stress. It has been reported that manic episodes may be preceded by elevated cortisol and adrenocorticotropic hormone (ACTH), and manipulation of the HPA axis may be a beneficial therapeutic strategy

Circadian Rhythms and Circadian Function
There are many rhythms in the human body that approximate to 24 hours. These are called circadian (circa dies = approximately 1 day) rhythms and can be found in many chemical systems including neurotransmitter metabolism. The central "clock" is found in the suprachiasmatic nucleus, a distinct group of cells in the hypothalamus. Since disruption in circadian function is known to occur in bipolar patients, it is possible that there is an association between the disruption of circadian function and the pathogenesis of the disease.

Glossary

Acetylcholine (ACh) — A neurotransmitter.

Acetylcholinesterase (AChE) — An enzyme whose function is to break down acetylcholine so that it becomes ineffective as a neurotransmitter. Conversely, when this enzyme is inhibited (see acetylcholinesterase inhibitors), the efficacy of acetylcholine is enhanced.

Acetycholinesterase Inhibitors — A class of drugs whose function is to inhibit the activity of acetylcholinesterase and so enhance the efficacy of acetylcholine as a neurotransmitter.

Advance Directive — A legal document that indicates the type of medical care a person wants to receive once they can no longer make or express these decisions due to incapacity. Two common forms of advance directive are Living Will and Durable Power of Attorney for Health Care.

Antidepressant(s) — Drugs designed to treat or alleviate the symptoms of unipolar (clinical) depression.

Antipsychotics — A class of drugs that alleviate the symptoms of psychotic behaviors, such as schizophrenia, and help to prevent or reduce the severity of the symptoms of mania.

Atrophy — Decrease in size or wasting away of a body part or tissue.

Biochemical Marker — Used to track the course of the disease and may provide a diagnostic test for the disease. A biochemical compound is identified whose concentrations change in relation to a critical pathogenic feature of the disease. For biochemical markers to be useful in everyday clinical situations, it is essential that the sensitivity and specificity are the same early on in the course of bipolar disorder and later in disease progression.

Bipolar I — One or more manic episodes or mixed episodes and often one or more major depressive episodes. Depressive episodes may last for several weeks or months, alternating with intense symptoms of mania that may last just as long. Between episodes, there may be periods of normal functioning. Symptoms may also be related to seasonal changes.

Bipolar II — One or more major depressive episodes accompanied by at least one hypomanic episode. Between episodes, there may be periods of normal functioning. Symptoms may also be related to seasonal changes.

Bipolar Disorder Not Otherwise Specified (NOS) — When a person displays the symptoms of a manic episode and a major depressive episode, but does not fit into the diagnosis of bipolar I, bipolar II, or cyclothymia, they are diagnosed as bipolar disorder NOS.

Bipolar Spectrum Disorder — A form of bipolar disorder that has been proposed (not accepted) where no manic or hypomanic episodes exist.

Butyrylcholinesterase (BuChE) — An enzyme found in human brain neurons and glia. The activity of BuChE in the brain increases with age (>60 years).

Butyrylcholinesterase Inhibitors — A class of drugs that inhibits butyrylcholinesterase in the brain.

Central Nervous System (CNS) — The brain and spinal cord. The brain is further divided into the cerebrum, diencephalon, basal ganglia, brainstem, and cerebellum.

Cerebrospinal Fluid (CSF) — A fluid found in the brain and spinal cord that serves to maintain a uniform pressure within the central nervous system.

Cholinesterase Inhibitors — See Acetylcholinesterase Inhibitors and Butyrylcholinesterase Inhibitors.

Combination Therapy — Two or more drugs when used in combination have a more beneficial effect than either drug alone.

Comorbidity — Pathological or disease conditions that are unrelated to the primary disease (bipolar disorder in this case), but occur at the same time.

Computed Tomography (CT) — A method of examining body organs by scanning them with X-rays and using a computer to construct a series of cross-sectional scans along a single axis.

Cortex — The outer layer of grey matter (unmyelinated neurons) that covers the cerebral hemispheres of the brain.

Cyclothymia (Cyclothymic Disorder) — Characterized by chronic fluctuating moods involving periods of hypomania and depression. The periods of both depressive and hypomanic symptoms are shorter, less severe, and do not occur with regularity as experienced with bipolar II or I disorders. However, these mood swings can impair social interactions and work. Many, but not all, people with cyclothymia develop a more severe form of bipolar illness.

Delusion — A false belief regarding the self, or persons or objects outside the self, that persists despite the facts.

Dementia — Deterioration of intellectual faculties, such as memory, concentration, and judgment, resulting from an organic disease or a disorder of the brain. It is sometimes accompanied by emotional disturbance and personality changes.

Depression/Major Depressive Episode — A period during which there is either depressed mood or the loss of interest or pleasure in nearly all activities, lasting for at least 2 weeks.

DNR — Do not resuscitate.

Dopamine — A monoamine neurotransmitter found in the brain and essential for the normal functioning of the central nervous system.

DSM-IV — The Diagnostic and Statistical Manual of Mental Disorders - Fourth Edition

Durable Power of Attorney for Health Care — A document that allows the patient to appoint a person (spouse, trusted family member, or friend) to make decisions about the patient's care and treatment. See also Medical Power of Attorney and Health Care Surrogate.

Gene Therapy — The insertion of genetically altered genes into cells to replace defective genes or to provide a specific disease-fighting function.

Glia — Cells that provide metabolic support and immune protection for neurons.

Grey Matter — Forms the superficial parts of the brain and the deep parts of the spinal cord and is comprised of many nerve cell bodies and few myelinated axons. Responsible for information processing.

Hallucination — The visual perception of an object that is not present.

Health Care Surrogate — A person appointed to make health care decisions for the patient when they become unable to make such decisions for themselves. The patient has no say in who becomes their health care surrogate. The patient can avoid having a health care surrogate appointed by appointing a medical power of attorney while they are able. See also Medical Power of Attorney.

Hippocampus — A ridge in the floor of each lateral ventricle of the brain that consists mainly of grey matter and has a central role in memory processes. A part of the limbic system.

Homeostasis — The maintenance of relatively stable internal physiological conditions (as body temperature or the pH of blood) in higher animals under fluctuating environmental conditions.

Hypersomnia — An excessive amount of sleepiness, resulting in an inability to stay awake.

Hypomania — A milder form of mania that lasts at least 4 days. Hypomanic episodes have symptoms similar to manic episodes, but are less severe, and are clearly different from a person's nondepressed mood. For some, hypomanic episodes are not severe enough to cause notable problems in social activities or work.

Insomnia — Inability to sleep or stay asleep for a reasonable period.

Living Will — Written instructions that state the individual's preferences about the kinds of life-sustaining treatments they would or would not want to have, and which should be withdrawn or withheld if the patient is terminally ill or facing imminent death.

LLD — Late-life depression.

Magnetic Resonance Imaging (MRI) — The use of a nuclear magnetic resonance spectrometer to produce electronic images of specific atoms and molecular structures in solids, especially human cells, tissues, and organs.

Mania/Manic Episode — Full-blown mania with delusions. A distinct period during which there is an abnormally and constantly elevated, expansive, or irritable mood, lasting at least 1 week.

Medicaid — A program providing medical care for the needy under joint federal and state participation in the United States.

Medical Power of Attorney — A person appointed to make health care decisions for the patient after they become unable to make such decisions for themselves. They can specify what health care decisions their medical power of attorney can make.

Medicare — A federally sponsored health insurance and medical program for persons 65 and older in the United States.

Medigap — Private health insurance designed to supplement the coverage provided under governmental programs such as Medicare in the United States.

Memory (Immediate) — Type of memory in which information is remembered for only a few seconds.

Memory (Long-Term) — Memory that involves the storage and recall of information over a long period of time (as days, weeks, or years).

Memory (Remote) — Memory for things that happened in the distant past that are remembered long term.

Memory (Short-Term) — Memory that involves recall of information for a relatively short time (a few minutes or hours).

Mixed Episode — A period of time during which a person experiences both manic and major depressive symptoms nearly every day for at least 1 week.

Motormental Retardation — See Psychomotor Retardation.

MRI — See Magnetic Resonance Imaging.

Myelin — A white fatty material composed chiefly of alternating layers of lipids and lipoproteins that encloses the axons of myelinated nerve fibers.

Neuroglia — See Glia.

Neuroleptic — A tranquilizing drug, especially one used in treating mental disorders.

Neuron — A cell that is specialized to conduct nerve impulses in the central nervous system and the peripheral nervous system.

Neurodevelopment (neural development) — the cellular and molecular mechanisms by which complex nervous systems emerge during embryonic development and throughout life.

Neurodegeneration — the progressive loss of structure or function of neurons, including death of neurons.

Neurotransmitter — Any of the various chemical substances, such as acetylcholine, glutamate, norepinephrine, serotonin, that transmit nerve impulses across a synapse.

NMDA — N-methyl-D-aspartate.
NMDA Receptor Antagonists — A class of drugs that work by blocking the NMDA receptor at nerve synapses.

Norepinephrine (Noradrenaline) — Catecholamine that is the chemical means of transmission across synapses in postganglionic neurons of the sympathetic nervous system and in some parts of the central nervous system, is a vasopressor hormone of the adrenal medulla, and is a precursor of epinephrine.

Pathophysiology — The functional changes or the study of such changes associated with or resulting from disease or injury.

Peripheral Nervous System — All nervous structures outside the central nervous system. Includes the cranial nerves that supply the head and neck, spinal nerves that supply the trunk and extremities, and the autonomic nervous system (ANS) that supplies the smooth muscle and glands of internal organs.

Phagocytes — specialized cells that serve to remove debris and foreign bodies and thus fight infection by the process known as phagocytosis whereby the debris or bacteria are enveloped by a membrane and internalized by the phagocyte. There are several kinds of phagocytic cells in the human body.

Positron Emission Tomography (PET) — Tomography in which a computer-generated image of a biological activity within the body is produced through the detection of gamma rays that are emitted when introduced radionuclides decay and release positrons.

Power of Attorney (POA) — A legal document that gives another person the authority to manage the patient's property.

Prodromal — Symptomatic of the onset of an attack or a disease.

Psychomotor Agitation — Involves purposeless motion that usually stems from mental tension of the individual. This could include pacing about a room in a specific path, the wringing of one's hands, pulling clothing off and putting it back on, and similar actions.

Psychomotor Retardation — Comprises a slowing down of thought and a reduction of physical movement. Often accompanied by psychosis.

Psychosis — Loss of contact with reality. A generic term for a mental state in which thought and perception are severely impaired.

Psychotropic — Exerting an effect on the mind or mental capacities.

Rapid Cycling — When the change in mood occurs frequently, at least four episodes within a 12-month period, it is referred to as "rapid cycling" and is more common in women and children than men. Some people experience multiple episodes within a single week or even within a single day. Rapid cycling tends to develop in the later stages of bipolar disorder.

Serotonin — A neurotransmitter involved in sleep, depression, and memory.

Single Photon Emission Computed Tomography (SPECT) — Similar to X-ray computed tomography (CT) or magnetic resonance imaging (MRI), SPECT allows us to visualize functional information about a patient's specific organ or body system. Internal radiation is administered by means of a pharmaceutical, which is labeled with a radioactive isotope. This so-called radiopharmaceutical, or tracer, is either injected, ingested, or inhaled. The radioactive isotope decays, resulting in the emission of gamma rays. These gamma rays give us a picture of what is happening inside the patient's body.

SNRI (Serotonin Norepinephrine Reuptake Inhibitor) — A class of antidepressant drugs that work by increasing the levels of serotonin and norepinephrine in the brain.

SSRI (Selective Serotonin Reuptake Inhibitor) — A class of antidepressant drugs that work by increasing the levels of serotonin in the brain.

Synapse — The junction across which a nerve impulse passes from an axon terminal to a neuron, a muscle cell, or a gland cell. Nerve impulses cross a synapse through the action of neurotransmitters.

Thalamus — The thalamus is a part of the brain. The two thalami are located in the center of the brain, one beneath each cerebral hemisphere and next to the third ventricle. Functionally, the thalami can be thought of as relay stations for nerve impulses carrying sensory information into the brain. The thalami receive these sensory inputs as well as inputs from other parts of the brain and determine which of these signals to forward to the cerebral cortex.

Tomography — Methods of obtaining pictures of the interior of the body.

Unipolar Depression (Clinical Depression) — A state of sadness or despair that is disruptive to a person's social functioning and activities of daily living.

Ventricle — Any of the interconnecting cavities of the brain that are continuous with the central canal of the spinal cord and contain cerebrospinal fluid.

White Matter — Composed of myelinated axons and connects various grey matter areas of the brain to each other and carries nerve impulses between neurons. Responsible for information transmission.

Printed in the United States
92910LV00002B/108/A